a-ha
The Story So Far . . .

Tor Marcussen

ZOMBA BOOKS

red herring

This edition first published in Great Britain in 1986 by Zomba Books, Zomba House, 165-167 Willesden High Road, London NW10 2SG, in association with Red Herring Publishing Ltd, 83/84 Long Acre, London WC2E 9NG.

ISBN 0 946391 83 1

Text by Tor Marcussen.

Designed by Tor Ditlefsen.

Cover designed by Clive Dorman.

Typeset by Island Graphics, Chesham, Bucks.

Printed in Belgium by Henri Proost & CIE PVBA.

Photographs on pp. 2, 6, 10, 26, 28, 30, 31, 33, 34, 35, 40, 41, 42, 44, 46, 60, 64, 77 and 80 courtesy of Rolf Aagaard.
Photographs on pp. 36, 37, 38, 39, 68, 72, 73, 74 and 79 courtesy of Tor Marcussen.
Photographs on pp. 4, 23, 48, 52 and 56 courtesy of Robert Erdmann (W.B.).
Bridges photographs courtesy of Henning Kramer Dahl.

First published in Norway by Chr. Schibsteds Forlag, Oslo in 1985.

a-ha *The Story So Far . . .*

Contents

Introduction — A Book About A Norwegian Pop Group?

New York, 1985. From left to right: Pal Waaktaar, Tor Marcussen, Morten Harket and Mags Furuholmen.

8

Why not, after all the story of their international success reads like a fairy tale, but it's true! They have managed what countless other Norwegian artists can only dream of. Rather than complaining about the restricted market, the provincial conditions and the lack of vision to be found in Norway, *a*-h*a* took matters into their own hands and did what the others just talk about - went abroad, got signed up, made a record and topped the charts all over the world!

The story of *a*-h*a* is also the story of a generation with self-confidence. Pal Waaktaar and Mags Furuholmen decided to go to England and become pop musicians before they even reached their teens. Morten Harket has always had his head in the clouds - but now even his most unrealistic dreams are coming true.

Dreams have become reality for *a*-h*a* because they believe in themselves. They don't have to resort to drugs to deal with reality. They get high on creativity, love and individualism. And they've achieved their success not by stabbing people in the back, but by relying on loyalty and responsibility.

As for myself, I was lucky enough to be around when all this success started to happen for them. The boys in the band managed to talk my way into, not only Warner Brothers' offices, but to private parties with Elton John and Dionne Warwick. I joined *a*-h*a* on their first big promotional tour, from Los Angeles to New York, from London to Sydney. And I got to know three distinct individuals who were not only concerned with their own careers, but unselfishly helped and supported one another and a poor, hard-working journalist.

Pal, Mags and Morten always found room to squeeze one more into the limousine, while the record company representatives, who are hired to protect stars from journalists such as myself, were tearing their hair out. In the middle of an inhuman schedule the boys found time for several hour-long interviews where they openly shared their innermost thoughts and feelings. And I was able to take part in personal celebrations as well as private, unofficial discussions about everything from finances to intimate affairs. I gained an insight into the international promotion of a new group as I was allowed to attend planning meetings, discussions about new videos, financing and promotional schemes – at a level where 'gentlemen of the press' are seldom welcomed.

There had to be a book about *a-ha* because they deserve more than just articles in magazines and newspapers. The book tries to recreate the atmosphere during the months when everything exploded, and to give a more detailed description of the history of *a-ha*'s origins and of the three boys' personal backgrounds than a newspaper column permits.

Thanks to Pal, Mags and Morten and to manager Terry Slater for making it possible for me to obtain the material for this book, and for having taken the time to read through the manuscript. Without their co-operation this project would have been impossible.

Tor Marcussen

About the author

Tor Marcussen graduated as a psychologist before becoming a full-time writer. For the last eight years he has worked for Aftenposten, Norway's leading daily newspaper, as a music critic and journalist.

a-ha: the story so far . . . is Tor's first solo book. He wrote it as a result of the encouragement he received from Pal, Morten and Mags right from the beginning of the tour.

Tor has travelled extensively for his newspaper covering such events as the Rock in Rio Festival and the Michael Jackson 'Victory' Tour in the USA.

Among the stars he has interviewed are: Bruce Springsteen, Bob Dylan, Mick Jagger, Bob Marley, Paul McCartney, ABBA, David Bowie, Chuck Berry, Rod Stewart, Boy George, Elton John and many, many others.

Tor has become a good friend of the boys and looks forward to covering their future successes.

A Night to remember 11
Number One In The USA!

"Isn't there anything better on TV?" snarls Mags as he switches from channel to channel, finding nothing but tacky soaps, boring chat shows and dull films. Maybe it's just that the boys are tired. Another hard working day is over, and tomorrow morning they'll be getting up early to finish the video production of *The Sun Always Shines On TV*. The director, Steve Barron, is an incredibly hard worker and demands rested actors - at an early hour.

It is October 9, 1985. We are sitting with a lukewarm Budweiser and a can of low-calorie Cola, staring at the garish colours on the TV screen. Morten is in his room. Pal is leafing through his notebook, jotting down loose thoughts and ideas and making sketches which may become new ideas, songs and lyrics. Mags and I are trying to follow what's on TV. It's only half past nine in the evening, but in the three-room apartment at the John Howard Hotel in Kensington, London, it's about time to call it a day. Clothes, letters and instruments lie strewn about the floor. Morten's girlfriend, Bunty, takes a friend of hers to the tube station. Pal stretches, looks at the clock and says, "I think I'll hit the sack".

Just then the telephone rings. "Oh, what now," groans Mags, who is sitting nearest the phone and picks it up to answer. Everything seems to go quiet, with only the noise of the TV droning on in the background. Until Mags explodes. Jumping about three feet in the air, he shouts, "We're number one in the USA!" The telephone falls to the floor, Pal tips his glass over on the table. Morten comes flying through the door, slamming it shut with a bang. The news from Los Angeles is true! *a-ha*'s first single, *Take On Me*, has gone to the top of the Billboard chart in the USA. The boys all start talking, laughing and crying at the same time. Everyone is hugging each other, and Bunty is nearly mowed down by them when she comes back from the tube. "We're number one! We're number one!"

Suddenly everyone starts diving for the telephone. I want to catch the newspapers before they go to print in Norway, and the others want to call Lauren in Boston, Heidi in Oslo, their mothers, fathers, grandparents and friends.

So, the evening is not over after all. What else could we do now but go out and celebrate! No time to order the usual limousines, so Bunty and I dive into a taxi and the boys bicker about which restaurant to go to. We end up in the West End, a part of town the boys know as well as Oslo, having spent several meagre years living in London. They charge about as if they were in a film, jumping over fire hydrants, congratulating total strangers on the street, racing each other, stopping cars, making faces, screaming and shouting. Finally we stumbled down the stairs to Joe Allen's restaurant in Covent Garden. The way is barred by a head waiter who is being bawled out by two customers complaining about the service. So we just force our way around the quarellers and seat ourselves at a corner table.

FOR WEEK ENDING OCTOBER 19, 1985

Billboard

HOT 100 SINGLES

Compiled from a national sample of retail store and one-stop sales reports and radio playlists.

THIS WEEK	LAST WEEK	2 WKS. AGO	WKS. ON CHART	TITLE / PRODUCER (SONGWRITER)	ARTIST / LABEL & NUMBER DISTRIBUTING LABEL
(1)	3	4	15	TAKE ON ME / A.TARNEY (P.WAAKTAAR, MAGS, N.HARKET) — 1 week at No. One	◆ A-HA / WARNER BROS. 7-29011
(2)	4	6	10	SAVING ALL MY LOVE FOR YOU / M.MASSER (M.MASSER, G.GOFFIN)	◆ WHITNEY HOUSTON / ARISTA 1-9381
(3)	5	10	7	PART-TIME LOVER / S.WONDER (S.WONDER)	STEVIE WONDER / TAMLA 1808/MOTOWN
4	1	3	12	OH SHEILA / READY FOR THE WORLD (M.RILEY, G.STROZIER, G.VALENTINE)	◆ READY FOR THE WORLD / MCA 52636
(5)	9	13	7	MIAMI VICE THEME / J.HAMMER (J.HAMMER)	JAN HAMMER / MCA 52666
(6)	6	8	9	LONELY OL' NIGHT / LITTLE BASTARD,D.GEHMAN (J.C.MELLENCAMP)	◆ JOHN COUGAR MELLENCAMP / RIVA 880-984-7/POLYGRAM
7	2	1	15	MONEY FOR NOTHING / M.KNOPFLER,N.DORFSMAN (M.KNOPFLER, STING)	◆ DIRE STRAITS / WARNER BROS. 7-28950
8	7	9	8	DANCING IN THE STREET / C.LANGER,A.WINSTANLEY (I.HUNTER, W.STEVENSON, M.GAYE)	◆ MICK JAGGER & DAVID BOWIE / EMI-AMERICA 8288
(9)	11	12	9	FORTRESS AROUND YOUR HEART / STING,P.SMITH (STING)	◆ STING / A&M 2767
(10)	13	20	6	HEAD OVER HEELS / C.HUGHES (ORZABEL, SMITH)	◆ TEARS FOR FEARS / MERCURY 880 899-7/POLYGRAM
(11)	12	14	7	I'M GOIN' DOWN / B.SPRINGSTEEN,J.LANDAU,C.PLOTKIN,S.VAN ZANDT (B.SPRINGSTEEN)	BRUCE SPRINGSTEEN / COLUMBIA 38-05603
(12)	15	19	9	LOVIN' EVERY MINUTE OF IT / T.ALLOM,P.DEAN (R.J.LANGE)	◆ LOVERBOY / COLUMBIA 38-05569
13	8	2	16	CHERISH / J.BONNEFORD,R.BELL,KOOL & THE GANG (R.BELL, J.TAYLOR, KOOL & THE GANG)	◆ KOOL & THE GANG / DE-LITE 880 869-7/POLYGRAM
14	10	5	10	DRESS YOU UP / N.RODGERS (P.STANZIALE, A.LARUSSO)	◆ MADONNA / SIRE 7-28919/WARNER BROS.
(15)	24	32	6	YOU BELONG TO THE CITY / G.FREY (G.FREY, J.TEMPCHIN)	GLENN FREY / MCA 52651
(16)	18	27	7	I'M GONNA TEAR YOUR PLAYHOUSE DOWN / L.LATHAM (E.RANDALL)	◆ PAUL YOUNG / COLUMBIA 38-05577
(17)	25	31	7	WE BUILT THIS CITY / P.WOLF,J.SMITH (B.TAUPIN, M.PAGE, D.LAMBERT, P.WOLF)	◆ STARSHIP / GRUNT 14170/RCA
(18)	23	28	9	BE NEAR ME / M.FRY,M.WHITE (M.FRY, M.WHITE)	◆ ABC / MERCURY 880 626-7/POLYGRAM
(19)	21	30	6	ONE NIGHT LOVE AFFAIR / B.ADAMS,B.CLEARMOUNTAIN (B.ADAMS, J.VALLANCE)	BRYAN ADAMS / A&M 2770
20	19	23	9	FOUR IN THE MORNING (I CAN'T TAKE ANYMORE) / P.GLASSER (J.BLADES)	◆ NIGHT RANGER / CAMEL/MCA 52661/MCA
(21)	29	36	7	YOU ARE MY LADY / B.EASTMOND (B.EASTMOND)	◆ FREDDIE JACKSON / CAPITOL 5495
(22)	26	29	8	SUNSET GRILL / D.HENLEY,D.KORTCHMAR,G.LADANYI (D.HENLEY, D.KORTCHMAR, TENCH)	DON HENLEY / GEFFEN 7-28906/WARNER BROS.
(23)	28	33	11	AND WE DANCED / R.CHERDOFF (R.HYMAN, E.BAZILIAN)	◆ THE HOOTERS / COLUMBIA 38-05568
(24)	30	34	5	LAY YOUR HANDS ON ME / A.SADKIN,N.RODGERS,T.BAILEY (T.BAILEY, A.CURRIE, J.LEEWAY)	◆ THE THOMPSON TWINS / ARISTA 1-9396
25	14	7	13	FREEDOM / G.MICHAEL (G.MICHAEL)	◆ WHAM! / COLUMBIA 38-05409
(26)	32	39	9	LOVE THEME FROM ST. ELMO'S FIRE (INSTRUMENTAL) / D.FOSTER,H.GATICA (D.FOSTER)	DAVID FOSTER / ATLANTIC 7-89528
(27)	33	38	6	NEVER / R.NEVISON (KNIGHT, BLOCH, CONNIE)	◆ HEART / CAPITOL 5512
(28)	35	41	4	WHO'S ZOOMIN' WHO / N.M.WALDEN (N.M.WALDEN, P.GLASS, A.FRANKLIN)	ARETHA FRANKLIN / ARISTA 9410
(29)	37	45	3	SEPARATE LIVES (THEME FROM WHITE NIGHTS) / A.MARDIN,P.COLLINS (S.BISHOP)	◆ PHIL COLLINS/MARILYN MARTIN / ATLANTIC 7-89498
30	17	16	14	CRY / T.HORN,GODLEY&CREME (GODLEY & CREME)	◆ GODLEY & CREME / POLYDOR 881 786-7/POLYGRAM
31	20	24	8	THE WAY YOU DO THE THINGS YOU DO/MY GIRL / D.HALL,J.OATES,B.CLEARMOUNTAIN (W.ROBINSON,JR., R.ROGERS)	◆ DARYL HALL & JOHN OATES / RCA 14178
32	16	11	14	DON'T LOSE MY NUMBER / P.COLLINS,H.PADGHAM (P.COLLINS)	◆ PHIL COLLINS / ATLANTIC 7-89536
(33)	36	40	6	BOY IN THE BOX / P.CHAPMAN,J.ASTLEY,C.HART (C.HART)	◆ COREY HART / EMI-AMERICA 8287
34	34	37	7	COMMUNICATION / B. EDWARDS (D.BRAMBLE, R.PALMER, A.TAYLOR, J.TAYLOR)	THE POWER STATION / CAPITOL 5511
(35)	41	50	5	BROKEN WINGS / P.DEVILLIERS,MR.MISTER (R.PAGE, S.GEORGE, J.LANG)	◆ MR. MISTER / RCA 14136
(36)	39	44	8	SO IN LOVE / S.HAGUE (O.M.D., S.HAGUE)	◆ ORCHESTRAL MANOEUVERS IN THE DARK / A&M/VIRGIN 2746/A&M
(37)	40	52	3	ONE OF THE LIVING / M.CHAPMAN (H.KNIGHT)	◆ TINA TURNER / CAPITOL 5518
38	22	18	11	C-I-T-Y / K.VANCE (J.CAFFERTY)	◆ JOHN CAFFERTY/BEAVER BROWN BAND / SCOTTI BROS. 4-05452/EPIC
39	27	15	18	ST. ELMO'S FIRE (MAN IN MOTION) / D.FOSTER (D.FOSTER, J.PARR)	◆ JOHN PARR / ATLANTIC 7-89541
40	31	17	15	DARE ME / R.PERRY (S.LORBER, D.INNIS)	◆ THE POINTER SISTERS / RCA 14126
(41)	50	59	7	PERFECT WAY / GREEN,GAMSON,MAHER (GREEN, GAMSON)	◆ SCRITTI POLITTI / WARNER BROS. 7-28949
(42)	52	72	3	GIRLS ARE MORE FUN / R.PARKER,JR. (R.PARKER,JR.)	RAY PARKER JR. / ARISTA 1-9352
(43)	53	65	3	THE NIGHT IS STILL YOUNG / P.RAMONE (B.JOEL)	BILLY JOEL / COLUMBIA 38-05657
(44)	54	63	3	SOUL KISS / J.FARRAR (M.GOLDENBERG)	◆ OLIVIA NEWTON-JOHN / MCA 52686
45	45	51	8	WEIRD SCIENCE / D.ELFMAN,S.BARTEK (D.ELFMAN)	◆ OINGO BOINGO / MCA 52633
(46)	49	56	6	I MISS YOU / KLYMAXX,L.MALSBY (L.MALSBY)	KLYMAXX / MCA/CONSTELLATION 52606/MCA
47	44	49	13	TONIGHT IT'S YOU / J.DOUGLASS (R.NIELSEN, R.ZANDER, J.ZANDER, J.BRANDT, M.RADICE)	◆ CHEAP TRICK / EPIC 34-05431
48	48	54	5	BORN IN EAST L.A. / J.EYRICH (B.SPRINGSTEEN, CHEECH & CHONG)	◆ CHEECH & CHONG / MCA 52655
(49)	NEW ▶			SLEEPING BAG / B.HAM (GIBBONS, HILL, BEARD)	Z Z TOP / WARNER BROS. 7-28884
50	38	26	17	THE POWER OF LOVE / HUEY LEWIS & NEWS (C.HAYES, H.LEWIS, J.COLLA)	◆ HUEY LEWIS & THE NEWS / CHRYSALIS 4-42876
(51)	57	58	8	STAND BY ME / M.WHITE,R.BUCHANAN (B.E.KING, J.LEIBER, M.STOLLER)	◆ MAURICE WHITE / COLUMBIA 38-05571
(52)	NEW ▶			ALIVE & KICKING / J.IOVINE,B.CLEARMOUNTAIN (SIMPLE MINDS)	SIMPLE MINDS / A&M 2783
53	51	55	9	ALL OF ME FOR ALL OF YOU / DIMPLES (DIMPLES, B.WILSON, J.SKLAIR)	◆ 9.9 / RCA 14082
(54)	56	64	4	LIKE TO GET TO KNOW YOU WELL / R.HINE (H.JONES)	◆ HOWARD JONES / ELEKTRA 7-69598
(55)	58	62	6	AFTER THE FIRE / A.SHACKLOCK (P.TOWNSHEND)	◆ ROGER DALTREY / ATLANTIC 7-89491
56	46	47	8	YOU WEAR IT WELL / E.DEBARGE (C.DEBARGE, E.DEBARGE)	EL DEBARGE WITH DEBARGE / GORDY 1804GF/MOTOWN
(57)	63	70	7	RUNNING UP THAT HILL / K.BUSH (K.BUSH)	◆ KATE BUSH / EMI-AMERICA 8285
(58)	66	76	4	I'LL BE GOOD / B.WATSON,B.SWEDIEN,RENE & ANGELA (R.MOORE, A.WINBUSH)	◆ RENE & ANGELA / MERCURY 884 009-7/POLYGRAM
59	42	21	13	POP LIFE / PRINCE & REVOLUTION (PRINCE & REVOLUTION)	PRINCE & THE REVOLUTION / PAISLEY PARK 7-28998/WARNER BROS.
60	61	69	4	OBJECT OF MY DESIRE / K.DIAMOND,L.JOB (K.ADEYEMO, E.PHILLIPS, K.DIAMOND)	◆ STARPOINT / ELEKTRA 7-69621
61	43	22	16	WE DON'T NEED ANOTHER HERO (THUNDERDOME) / T.BRITTEN (T.BRITTEN, G.LYLE)	◆ TINA TURNER / CAPITOL 5491
(62)	NEW ▶			SISTERS ARE DOING IT FOR THEMSELVES / D.A.STEWART (LENNOX, STEWART)	EURYTHMICS AND ARETHA FRANKLIN / RCA 14214
63	64	68	4	SCREAMS OF PASSION / DAVID Z.,THE FAMILY (ST.PAUL, SUSANNAH)	◆ THE FAMILY / PAISLEY PARK 7-28953/WARNER BROS.
(64)	69	79	7	AND SHE WAS / TALKING HEADS (D.BYRNE)	◆ TALKING HEADS / SIRE 7-28917/WARNER BROS.
65	65	66	6	ALL FALL DOWN / N.MARTINELLI (B.BLUE, R.SMITH)	◆ FIVE STAR / RCA 14108
(66)	72	82	3	PARTY ALL THE TIME / R.JAMES (R.JAMES)	◆ EDDIE MURPHY / COLUMBIA 38-25609
67	47	25	11	EVERY STEP OF THE WAY / J.WAITE,S.GALFAS (J.WAITE, KRAL, SIDGWICK)	◆ JOHN WAITE / EMI-AMERICA 8282
68	70	83	4	THE OAK TREE / M.DAY (M.DAY)	◆ MORRIS DAY / WARNER BROS. 7-28899
69	71	73	5	HARD TIMES FOR LOVERS / A.BAKER,R.SCHER,L.GOLDEN (R.SCHER, L.GOLDEN)	JENNIFER HOLLIDAY / GEFFEN 7-28958/WARNER BROS.
(70)	NEW ▶			AMERICA / PRINCE & REVOLUTION (PRINCE & REVOLUTION)	PRINCE & THE REVOLUTION / PAISLEY PARK 7-28999/WARNER BROS.
(71)	84	—	2	TO LIVE AND DIE IN L.A. / T.SWAIN,S.JOLLEY (WANG CHUNG)	◆ WANG CHUNG / GEFFEN 7-28891/WARNER BROS.
72	60	43	18	FREEWAY OF LOVE / N.M.WALDEN (N.M.WALDEN, J.COHEN)	◆ ARETHA FRANKLIN / ARISTA 1-9354
(73)	76	81	5	HURTS TO BE IN LOVE / G.VANNELLI,J.VANNELLI,R.VANNELLI (G.VANNELLI)	◆ GINO VANNELLI / CBS ASSOCIATED 4-05586/EPIC
(74)	78	86	4	EYE TO EYE / G.STEVENSON,THE SYSTEM (P.COX, R.DRUMMIE)	GO WEST / CHRYSALIS VS4-42903
(75)	85	—	2	QUE TE QUIERO / KATRINA & WAVES (KATRINA & WAVES, P.COLLIER)	◆ KATRINA AND THE WAVES / CAPITOL 5528
(76)	82	89	3	KAYLEIGH / C.KIMSEY (MARILLION)	◆ MARILLION / CAPITOL 5493
77	79	85	4	BLUE KISS / G.MASSENBURG,B.PAYNE,R.KUNKEL (KIRSCH, WIEDLIN)	◆ JANE WIEDLIN / I.R.S. 52674/MCA
78	75	75	5	LOVER COME BACK TO ME / M.STOCK,M.AITKIN (DEAD OR ALIVE)	◆ DEAD OR ALIVE / EPIC 34-05607
79	77	80	5	EATEN ALIVE / B.GIBB,M.JACKSON,K.RICHARDSON,A.GALUTEN (B.GIBB, M.GIBB, M.JACKSON)	◆ DIANA ROSS / RCA 14181
(80)	NEW ▶			TARZAN BOY / M.BASSI (N.HACKETT, M.BASSI)	◆ BALTIMORA / MANHATTAN 50018/CAPITOL
(81)	83	90	3	REMO'S THEME (WHAT IF) / T.SHAW,R.CANNATA (T.SHAW, R.CANNATA)	◆ TOMMY SHAW / A&M 2773
(82)	87	—	2	EVERYBODY DANCE / J.JOHNSON (J.JOHNSON, TAMARA)	TA MARA & THE SEEN / A&M 2768
83	55	35	16	INVINCIBLE (THEME FROM THE LEGEND OF BILLIE JEAN) / M.CHAPMAN (H.KNIGHT, S.CLIMIE)	◆ PAT BENATAR / CHRYSALIS 4-42877
(84)	NEW ▶			HOLD ME / J.WHITE,H.FALTERMEYER (B.ANDERSEN, B.BODINE)	LAURA BRANIGAN / ATLANTIC 7-89496
(85)	NEW ▶			TEARS ARE FALLING / P.STANLEY,G.SIMMONS (P.STANLEY)	◆ KISS / MERCURY 884 141-7/POLYGRAM
86	59	42	13	I GOT YOU BABE / UB40,R.P.FALCONER (S.BONO)	◆ UB40 / A&M 2758
87	73	67	20	I WONDER IF I TAKE YOU HOME / FULL FORCE (FULL FORCE)	◆ LISA LISA/CULT JAM WITH FULL FORCE / COLUMBIA 38-04886
88	68	53	17	SUMMER OF '69 / B.ADAMS,B.CLEARMOUNTAIN (B.ADAMS, J.VALLANCE)	◆ BRYAN ADAMS / A&M 2739
(89)	NEW ▶			WELCOME TO PARADISE / J.WAITE,S.GALSAS (J.WAITE)	JOHN WAITE / EMI-AMERICA 8278
(90)	NEW ▶			TALK TO ME / S.LEVINE (M.ROSS, R.ROSS)	QUARTERFLASH / GEFFEN 7-289087/WARNER BROS.
91	88	—	2	I'LL BE THERE / K.LOGGINS (K.LOGGINS, D.FOSTER, E.E.LOGGINS)	KENNY LOGGINS / COLUMBIA 38-05625
92	62	46	15	YOU'RE ONLY HUMAN (SECOND WIND) / P.RAMONE (B.JOEL)	◆ BILLY JOEL / COLUMBIA 38-05417
93	89	—	2	YOU'RE IN LOVE / B.HILL (PEARCY, CROUCIER)	◆ RATT / ATLANTIC 7-89502
94	67	48	15	SMOKIN' IN THE BOYS ROOM / T.WERMAN (M.LUTZ, C.KODA)	◆ MOTLEY CRUE / ELEKTRA 7-69625
(95)	NEW ▶			CONGA / E.ESTEFAN (E.E.GARCIA)	◆ MIAMI SOUND MACHINE / EPIC 34-05457
96	81	61	20	NEVER SURRENDER / P.CHAPMAN,J.ASTLEY,C.HART (C.HART)	◆ COREY HART / EMI-AMERICA 8268
97	90	78	21	WHAT ABOUT LOVE? / R.NEVISON (ALTON, ALLEN, VALLANCE)	◆ HEART / CAPITOL 5481
98	74	60	19	SHOUT / C.HUGHES (ORZABEL, STANLEY)	◆ TEARS FOR FEARS / MERCURY 880 294-7/POLYGRAM
99	86	74	16	LIFE IN ONE DAY / R.HINE (H.JONES)	◆ HOWARD JONES / ELEKTRA 7-69631
100	98	98	22	FOREVER / K.LOGGINS,D.FOSTER (K.LOGGINS, D.FOSTER)	◆ KENNY LOGGINS / COLUMBIA 38-04931

( ) Products with the greatest airplay and sales gains this week. ◆ Video clip availability. ● Recording Industry Assn. Of America (RIAA) seal for sales of one million units. ▲ RIAA seal for sales of two million units.

14

There's no doubt about what the appetizer will be: champagne! I am now about to witness a very special drinking session. Mags starts the ball rolling, and for once, the otherwise overly moderate Pal and Morten are game as well. "Bottoms Up!" shouts Pal, and down goes the second glass. He gives one more toast, then he slaps down his empty glass so that the stem splinters and the glass breaks. The pieces are deftly swept into the bottom of the champagne cooler before before the next bottle is ordered. Things calm down a bit now. The boys start to think about what has happened . . .

"It was unbelievable," says Pal. "It was as though my whole life flashed through my mind at once when I heard it."

"It sure feels great to have proof now that our expectations weren't too high, as so many people have told us," adds Mags.

The champagne is still flowing, but Morten and Bunty dilute it with orange juice and mineral water. And they pick soberly at their salads, while the rest of us gorge ourselves on steaks and gravy. It's not every day you're number one in the USA.

No one around us has any idea who it is sitting here celebrating so noisily. *a*-h*a* are not celebrities in England – yet. Scowls from the neighbouring table and a few snide comments from the waiters have no effect tonight. But when the bill arrives the situation does get somewhat embarrassing because the restaurant will not accept my American Express Card. So everyone empties their pockets and there's just enough left over for a small tip for the waiter.

"Hopefully we won't have to go through that next time we're number one," laughs Mags just before the cheerful gang heads back to the hotel. More hugs and congratulations and then to bed. But no. The grapevine and other, more technically advanced methods of spreading the news have been at work. Each and every newspaper office in Norway has grasped what has happened. So one by one, the Norwegian press comes streaming in, and the boys, being good patriots, go along with it. They're not likely to get much sleep before the alarm goes off in the morning to call them to their next video shoot. But it's unbelievable what you can handle when you know you're number one in the USA. The first big dream has come true, though not without a good deal of hard work.

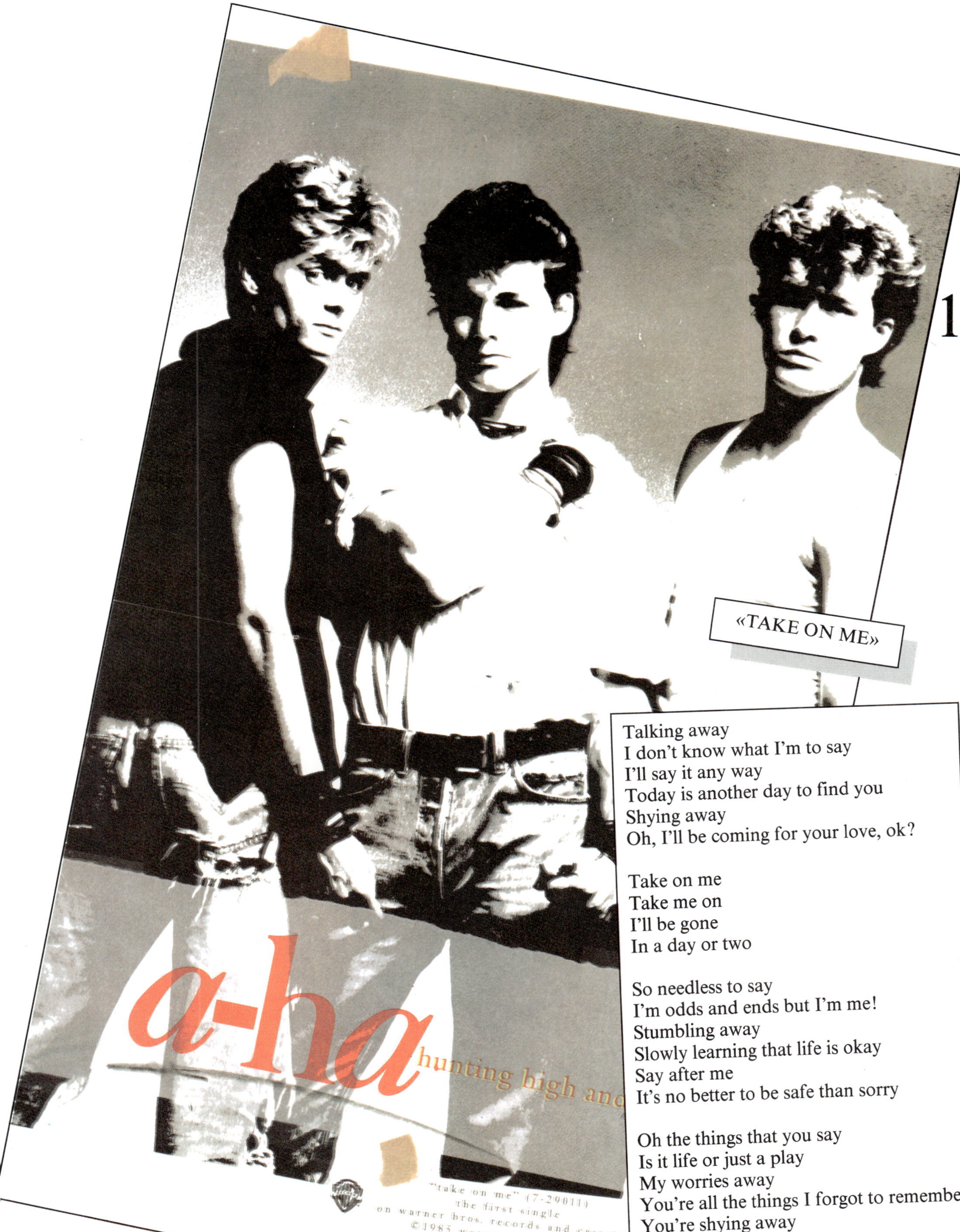

«TAKE ON ME»

Talking away
I don't know what I'm to say
I'll say it any way
Today is another day to find you
Shying away
Oh, I'll be coming for your love, ok?

Take on me
Take me on
I'll be gone
In a day or two

So needless to say
I'm odds and ends but I'm me!
Stumbling away
Slowly learning that life is okay
Say after me
It's no better to be safe than sorry

Oh the things that you say
Is it life or just a play
My worries away
You're all the things I forgot to remember
You're shying away
I'll be coming for you anyway

Take on Me (Pal Waaktaar/Magne Furuholmen/Morten Harket)

Mags, Morten and Pal —
a-ha set for success

The Early Years — Self-confidence, Determination and Lots of Hard Work.

17

The story of *a-ha* is the story of three Norwegian boys with will-power, idealism, a positive attitude towards life and their fair share of talent and good luck. It's been a long road from *a-ha*'s formation, via a cold cabin in Asker, Norway, and condemned flats in London, to their status as world stars. Pal and Mags began to play music together as ten and twelve year-olds. Two mates from the high-rises at Manglerud in Oslo. They started on recorders and tin plates and eventually graduated to guitars and cheap synthesizers. Pal had big ambitions from the very beginning and began composing at an early age, from simple melodies to rock operas. They played in different bands, and there was often competition between them which continued, even when they finally ended up in the same band.

Properly organised rehearsals as a group didn't start until their high school years. By then, Mags' family had moved to Asker (an area within commuting distance from Oslo) and Pal's parents had bought a summer

The first band, Bridges. Line-up from left to right, Viggo Bondi, Mags, Pal and Øystein Jevanord

The cover of Bridges' self financed LP

cabin in the same district. Asker thus become their base for practising and recruiting. Pal and Mags began to play in a band called Bridges, together with Viggo Bondi and Øystein Jevanord. Bridges played uncompromising, sometimes rather heavy music and their influence came from the leading USA group, The Doors, of whom Pal and Mags were both admirers.

After a while Bridges became too small-time for Pal and Mags. They had bigger ambitions than just playing at school parties or touring around Norway for that matter. They wanted to compete with the best, because they knew they were good. While other bands scraped together money to finance their own singles, in 1981 Bridges produced a whole LP, not with short, punky tracks, but with ambitious, almost symphonic pieces. All of the music was composed by the group themselves, most of it being written by Pal Waaktaar.

Pal and Mags realised that they had to do something unique in order to achieve success. Their music was so unusual that they felt they should address themselves to a much larger audience. They had to cultivate their ideas rather than impress listeners with brilliant playing techniques. So they palmed off the more simple synthesizers on the other two members of the band and went their own musical way. The others were not particularly pleased with the situation.

Simply, Pal and Mags wanted to go to England and the others did not. This ultimately led to a natural break-up. The two of them gradually

The boys get their act together! An early performance in front of a studio audience

discovered that between them they could manage the instrumental part of their music just fine. They could achieve the sound they wanted with drums, bass, guitars and synthesizers by themselves. But they needed a vocalist.

Morten Harket was a relatively new rock fan when he first heard Bridges play in Asker. He was impressed and got in contact with Viggo in order to get to know the boys in the group, but he didn't dare hint outright that maybe he would like to join them. After another gig he contacted Mags and they had a long, serious discussion while they walked the ten miles home from the Chateau Neuf concert hall in Oslo to Asker. They found they had a lot in common: in their philosophy of life; in their creative ideas.

At that time Morten was singing in a blues/soul band called Souldier Blue, led by Arild Fetveit. Mags had heard about Morten and knew that he sang well, but a long time went by after their 'serious talk' before Mags contacted him to find out if he would sing with them. But Morten was happy in Souldier Blue, and felt he didn't know enough about these impulsive creatures who were going to try their luck abroad. In the end Pal and Mags went to London on their own. They had a one-way ticket, the money they'd managed to save and the certainty that they were going to make it big.

But London and the 'big time' were not quite ready for the inexperienced, yet ambitious, duo. The only contact they had in England was a woman Mags knew, but unfortunately she lived in Birmingham . . .

After a while they found a cheap place to live in London. However, the 'flat', if you could call that one-room hole a flat, still cost money. The

£2,000 they had earned as a tram conductor and a substitute teacher in Norway was rapidly being swallowed up.

The boys advertised in Melody Maker for musicians to play with them. However, problems – financial and otherwise – were beginning to dominate their lives so there was little energy left for their music. Understandably enough they did not get a whole lot of response when people heard them, with Pal on acoustic guitar, Mags fumbling on a synth with a tiny amplifier and the two of them whistling the melodies. At one point one of their adverts was answered by a harpist, who stayed with them for a while . . . but it didn't lead to any great breakthrough! Time passed. Pal sat in the public library, read and tried to be creative. Mags sat in his room, watched TV and listened to the radio. He finally took a job in a pub, where he earned about one pound an hour, in order to try and get their funds to stretch a little further.

This lasted about six months, with numerous musicians moving in and out of the picture, creating lots of activity, but no results. So they decided to go back home and try to get Morten to join them. But they had no money for the trip, and had to hitchhike their way back . . . it rained the whole time.

Not only was the journey back to Norway long, tedious and wet, but, to cap it all, they got a fine for thumbing a lift on the motorway, just as they were walking over the border into Germany. Our young heroes were not feeling exactly on top of the world as they crossed the Svinesund bridge – on foot – in the summer of 1982, arriving back on Norwegian soil disillusioned and humiliated.

But Pal was not about to give up at this point. He intended to go right back to London - as soon as they could get Morten to join them. Morten was far more willing now, as he felt that the band he was with was in a period of stagnation. But he didn't want to go right away. He thought they should practise first and make some demonstration tapes so they would have something more than just their enthusiasm when they returned to London. After a heated discussion, Pal finally agreed to wait a couple of weeks – which became a month – which became two months – which turned into half a year. But they used the time well. They borrowed Pal's parents' summer cabin at Nernes in Asker, where they rigged up microphones, synths, tape recorders, cooking utensils and sleeping bags. They shut themselves away there, and finally things really started rolling. Pal got his ideas down on paper, Mags worked on the music, and Morten sang.

The first version of *Living A Boy's Adventure Tale* was put together at that time. Even more importantly, *Lesson One* took form, the song which would eventually become *Take On Me*. The boys lived in the cabin for weeks. It got cold as autumn came and their money for food dwindled. Pal and Mags helped themselves to plums from other people's gardens. Morten's principles wouldn't allow him to join them, but he was willing to make jam with the stolen fruit. The result was terrible. Sour and bitter. Morten claimed it was because the plums were stolen, while the others blamed it on too little sugar!

They stayed in the cabin until Christmas, but it grew too cold to continue living there. They were just about ready for the big move. Even Morten was now convinced that there was a future for the band – and not just in Norway. After the New Year's celebrations, Pal and Mags stayed up for two days and nights at a stretch in order to do the final mixing of the demo tapes. On 2 January 1983, Pal and Morten boarded the ferry, once again with one-way tickets to England. Mags came a week later as he wanted to spend some time with his girlfriend Heidi before leaving.

This is where to story of *a-ha* (as they had decided to call themselves) really begins. Originally, Pal had used the word 'a-ha' as the title of a song. He alternated between 'a-ha' and 'a-hem'. As Morten was taking one of his frequent peeks through Pal's notebook, he came across the name *a-ha*. "That's a great name. That's what we should call ourselves." After a few weeks of getting the feel of the name and checking dictionaries in several languages, it was decided. They found out that 'a-ha' was an international way of expressing recognition, with positive connotations. It was short, easy to say and unusual.

In January 1983 *a-ha* was ready for the 'big time' in England. They found a scruffy flat, bought the 'Virgin Yearbook of Rock' and 'Melody Maker's Yearbook' and then began calling record companies and publishing houses which dealt with song copyrights. The boys knew what they wanted, and they knew how to go about it this time. They needed no other musicians, they had eight songs on a demo tape, and the only thing they required now was a contract and the chance to record in a good studio. That couldn't take such a long time, could it?

It didn't go too badly to start with. They got an appointment with a man from Decca Record Company, who thought the music was good, but not good enough. No deal. Then they came in contact with a publishing house called Lionheart, who were seriously interested. There followed several auditions and lengthy negotiations.

Meanwhile, the boys were getting accustomed to London and acquiring a real taste for the big-city life. The day before they were to sign a contract with Lionheart, they went out on the town . . . and wound up with two Italian ladies in their flat. The Italian girls thought the Norwegian boys were really cute, and were interested in becoming more intimately acquainted. The boys were not. Morten and Pal tried frantically to talk themselves out of the situation. Mags' strategy was simply to hit the bottle! When the bottle was empty, and Mags fairly intoxicated, he decided to take matters into his own hands. He ran out into the street to get a taxi for the ladies. Charging full speed ahead down the road, he couldn't be bothered to slow down for a parked car directly in front of him. So he just ran straight over the car, landing, unfortunately, right on the head of a policeman. The otherwise fairly congenial English bobby is not quite so agreeable when a drunk Norwegian lands on his head! Mags' explanations were ignored, and he was subsequently thrown in jail and charged with disorderly conduct.

Pal and Morten finally got rid of the girls, and spent the rest of the night trying to locate Mags. The next morning, Morten showed up alone at the appointed time to sign the contract with Lionheart, while Pal was at the police station bailing out Mags – Mags having to declare himself guilty in order to get out. Meanwhile Morten was explaining their absence as being due to having so many other appointments, photo sessions, etc. .. So it was in these chaotic circumstances that *a-ha*'s first contract was signed. Lionheart was going to manage *a-ha*! But as Morten put his name to the contract he hoped and prayed that Mags had not been deported from the country just when the group's future seemed secured.

But their contract with Lionheart proved not to be the breakthrough they had hoped for. The company had neither the time nor the money to do much for *a-ha*. They had financial problems and furthermore were using all their time to pursue projects which were not proving to be commercial successes. Their only efforts on *a-ha*'s behalf were a few telephone calls at the end of the day – after their other business was taken care of. Naively,

a-ha had agreed to cancel all their other agreements to have a contract with Lionheart. So time was wasted, and *a-ha*'s money with it.

The boys were having a rough time. Their flat was a popular meeting place for the neighbourhood cats – and smelt like it. Electricity was paid for by inserting a token in a meter in the hallway. Often the boys missed the end of a TV film because the meter was empty and none of them had a token. They ended up with one light bulb that still worked in the flat. When one of the boys wanted to use the toilet, he had to unscrew the light bulb in the living room and take it into the bathroom. Their meals consisted of home-baked bread made from ingredients of suspect origin, with salt and pepper as sandwich-fillers. Pal lost over a stone in weight in the course of a few months, and the others were not much better off!

Boredom and disillusionment led inevitably to frayed tempers and arguments. On one occasion a friendly joke ended up as a fully-fledged row, with Mags eventually shoving Morten's head right through a window, shattering the glass.

Morten tried to get out of the claustrophobic atmosphere by hanging around with a new group of friends. For a while he lived with Steve Strange, a major influence in London's trendy fashion and music scene at the time. Here he was able both to eat fairly well for a few days and also be a passive observer of lifestyle quite different from his own miserable existence. But that didn't last long.

The boys went back to Norway for a short time to earn a bit more money. On their return to London they decided to give up on Lionheart, make some new and better demo tapes, and try again.

They scoured the music papers for adverts for small recording studios, and ended up with John Ratcliff's Rendezvous Studio, because it was the only studio that had both the equipment they needed – and the Space-Invaders game that Mags insisted on!

They booked the studio, intending to re-record five songs. After five intense days starting on 1 April 1983, they ended up with only two songs finished. At first John Ratcliff couldn't believe they had taken so long to produce so little output, but when he heard the songs beginning to take shape he had to agree that the result was encouraging. During a break in recording Morten had said "If these guys in the studio have ears, then they'll realise how great this is and come and help us out!" Twenty minutes later John Ratcliff came down and told them that although he had heard only a little of what they could do he was very impressed. Furthermore, he believed the band had a promising future and wanted to play the tapes to an influential friend in the record business. All of this on the basis of just two songs!

As it happened, out of the five songs that the boys had planned to re-record those two tracks have still not been released. The other three songs were, *Take on Me, Living a Boy's Adventure Tale* and *Train of Thought*! At this point *a*-h*a* were so disillusioned with Lionheart that they eagerly signed with John Ratcliff. John, in turn, introduced them to his friend and manager, Terry Slater. Terry was constantly being presented with new acts, but this time he realised that he had come across something special. He asked the boys to meet him at the famous Beatles studio in Abbey Road. He approved of the little he had already heard, but wanted to hear more before making a final decision. Could *a*-h*a* manage to finish a few more songs while he was spending a week in the USA?

With this encouragement, and £200 from John Ratcliff's otherwise tight pocket, the boys were inspired again. Among other songs which they managed to complete this time were *Take on Me* and *Living a Boy's Adventure Tale*. When Slater returned from the USA and listened to the songs, he lost all doubt. He formed T.J. Management with John Ratcliff, and – at last – *a*-h*a* had managers!

Now things started happening quickly, at least for a while. Slater proved to be an old hand at the music business, with contacts at the top of all the record companies. When he phoned around and informed them of his new 'act', they paid attention! *a*-h*a* set up in a little studio with their guitars and synthesizers, and played for everyone who would listen. One of the first on the scene was Andy Wickham, responsible for Warner Brothers' repertoire in England. He liked both the boys' music and their style. Instead of nervous and reserved performers, he found a relaxed and entertaining atmosphere. Wickham stayed long after his appointment was over. Warner Brothers were definitely interested!

Slater wanted to gamble for the highest stakes and invited representatives from the other important record companies. Not all of them were as enthusiastic as Andy Wickham, but only Slater and the boys knew that. So when the final decision time was approaching, Slater had his mates in other record companies call Warner Brothers to ask if they had signed up *a*-h*a* yet, because they were interested as well. As a result Warner Brothers increased their offer of advance royalties: first £25,000, then £50,000 up to £100,000 and finally £125,000. The contract was arranged directly with the head office in USA.

But the group's trials and tribulations were not quite over yet. Now the search began for the best producer and the best studio, and that took time. Terry Slater wanted Alan Tarney, an old friend who had worked wonders for the careers of artists like Cliff Richard and Leo Sayer. Tarney was a loner, with a clear sense of musical direction and he was sceptical about working with a band. He preferred solo artists, so he himself could control the musical aspect with a firm hand. The record company suggested many other names and ended up with Tony Mansfield, who was an expert in the use of computerised synthesizers. *a-ha* liked the idea and agreed.

Mansfield worked slowly. They started to fall behind schedule, and musically too, it wasn't working out. Mansfield took *a-ha*'s simple demos and turned on the machinery, filling the tapes with electronic gadgetry and mixing Morten's voice way back in the sound level. This was so far removed from what *a-ha* had hoped to achieve that, together with their old friend John Ratcliff, the lads had to remix the whole album again. All of this took time, which in the music business, means money. Financially, they were so far behind schedule that the co-operation between Terry Slater and Mansfield's manager collapsed once and for all. Eventually the album was finished, *Take On Me* released as a single in England and a video rushed through. And the result of all this activity and excitement? – nothing.

However, Warner Brothers' head office in the USA expressed an interest. They had heard about this promising Norwegian band, but where were the results? Important record company executives like Jeff Ayeroff became involved. The first video was canned and *a-ha* were given the opportunity to re-record *Take On Me*. Terry Slater managed to convince Alan Tarney to produce this one song and *a-ha* returned to the studio to record a rough cut of *Take On Me*. Tarney liked what he heard, but had to leave. While he was gone, Pal and Mags added more synthesizer to emphasise their original concept. When Tarney returned and heard the result, he said "Fine – that's just how it should be". "Then we'll do it for real," said Mags. "No, no – it's already done!" said Tarney. In no time they had completed the version of *Take On Me* that we all know and love. Warner Brothers' response was very enthusiastic – and immediately gave the go-ahead for another song, *The Sun Always Shines On TV*.

The album *Hunting High and Low* was now finished and the new version of *Take On Me* was re-released in England. However, the London office was so put out by the interference of the US that they gave absolutely no support to the release. The result was another flop.

To say that the boys were crushed is an understatement. The three idealists, who believed that talent alone would be enough to get them to the top, had now encountered so much adversity, wasted so much time, and been disappointed so often that they were on the point of giving up. They looked back on what it had taken to reach the position they were now in, and the people it had affected. John Ratcliff, who had risked everything for them, had ended up divorcing his wife, taking pills and drinking, and had such high blood pressure that he got a nosebleed just from talking to somebody. The pressure on Tony Mansfield from Warner Brothers had been such a burden that he almost had a break-down. They saw people's hopes, money and lives going to waste and decided to split up for a while.

Pal visited Lauren in Boston. He thought that *a-ha* were about to be kicked out of Warner Brothers for good, but since he was in the States he decided to check it out for himself, and gave them a call. Amazingly, the voice on the phone from Warner Brothers said, "It's great!" "We love *a-ha*, and you're now our top priority group! We're going to have a new video made of *Take on Me* and it's going to be fantastic!"

Optimism grew again, and with it more waiting. But this time they didn't wait in vain. When the new video of *Take on Me* was finished the USA suddenly lay wide open – it was sensational. The single was released three weeks after the video and immediately appeared in all the charts . . . and we know where it ended up. *a-ha* had done it!

ICE

We Want The World And We Want It Now . . .

World PR Tour

Live excitement in the studio at CBS. Paul Young is first in line for an interview. DJ Richard Blade introduces the boys on air

Making music, playing and recording, negotiating contracts . . . these are all just one side of being a pop artist. Equally important are public relations and using all the available media to inform people that "Here we are! We've got something special!". Warner Brothers and Terry Slater were experts at the game. They both made sure that all stops were pulled out: expensive videos, plenty of travelling, advertisements in the most influential magazines and newspapers, T-shirts with pictures of the boys, badges, posters, in other words, all the tricks of the trade.

So while the boys stayed at home in Oslo in August, 1985, eagerly following the slow climb of *Take on Me* from the bottom of the charts, after the release of the final version, Terry Slater was preparing for The Great Promotional Tour. At last, on 30 August, 1985, the boys flew to Los Angeles to participate in the growing excitement being generated in the USA around these unknown newcomers from the Arctic.

But first they had to get rid of their jet lag. The day is completely reversed between Oslo and Los Angeles. With the nine hour time difference, morning becomes evening and vice versa. After such long trips, Terry always gives the boys a few days to catch up before starting work again. So the first order of business is to check out the swimming pool at the Hotel Sheraton Universal, Burbank, Los Angeles. Margaritas with tequila, crushed ice and juice are followed by Mai Tais and other fancy drinks in every colour of the rainbow, then the jacuzzi beckons . . . delicious relaxation and recreation.

On Tuesday, 3 September it's down to serious business. A tightly packed schedule has been drawn up by Slater and Warner Brothers. Radio interviews, photographic sessions, video recordings, TV shows, meetings, newspaper interviews and a never ending list of other obligations.

Radio station KROQ is first on the list, chosen in gratitude for having been the first in the USA to start playing *Take on Me* regularly. It's an important radio station, always on the lookout for new groups.

Would-be pop stars have to be presented with style, and Warner Brothers certainly came up with the proper transportation – a long, lean, black limousine with colour TV, quadrophonic radio, a bar, and a licence plate which reads 'Music 24' delivers us to KROQ's not exactly plush offices and studios. Actually it's just a little closet, but disc jockey, Richard Blade, has already warmed up the atmosphere during a live broadcast, ready for *a-ha*'s appearance.

The parking lot is full of teenagers who scream and howl when Mags, Pal and Morten alight from their magnificent limousine and try to clear their way through the mad throng into the studio. The interview is presented live. In the midst of an organised chaos of microphones, records, cassettes, photographs, drawings and posters, as well as coffee cups, secretaries, dogs and neighbours, Richard Blade manages to orchestrate the disorderly proceedings perfectly to the second.

First he introduces the boys and plays *Take On Me*. Then they open the telephone lines, and within five seconds there are forty callers on the waiting list – girls, curious to know if the boys are married or have girlfriends, boys who wonder when they'll hold their first concert. One lucky caller is guaranteed to be the centre of attention in her classroom tomorrow after *a*-h*a* sing "Happy Birthday" to her in three-part harmony on the radio. But the studio will soon become even livelier: disc jockey, Blade, suddenly announces, "To you fans out in the parking lot – we're bringing five of you up to meet the boys!" And in march five giggling teenage girls who want hugs and autographs. More music follows and then *a*-h*a* are escorted back into their limousine.

Now we're on our way to the biggest radio station in Los Angeles: KIIS. Here they're a little more serious, but the questions are generally the same and the enthusiasm just as great.

Next stop, the CBS studios and their FM station. Here we have to wait our turn. Paul Young is facing the firing squad before *a*-h*a*. Later, we get to meet Paul who invites us all to his concert the next day and to the private party afterwards.

"Radio is important in the USA," says Slater afterwards, "Everyone listens to the radio while driving, and they're always driving!" Of course TV is important too. Slater has carefully chosen three nationally networked programmes for *a*-h*a*: Soul Train, Solid Gold and American Bandstand, which has broad youth appeal and approximately 25 million viewers. Soul Train is basically a black programme, and *a*-h*a* are in fact one of the very few white groups who have ever performed on it. Solid Gold, a programme dealing more with New Wave and Synth Pop, is first on the list.

Early on Wednesday morning the limousine floats into Universal Studios' heavily guarded complex. The excitement is palpable. It is *a*-h*a*'s first important TV slot. Millions of potential record buyers who want to find out more about this new group from Norway, will be watching. They've got to look good!

The tension mounts in the dressing-room as the boys wait for their cue. Finally presenter, Dionne Warwick thanks the professional, scantily-clad dancing group for the opening act and introduces *a*-h*a*. *Take on Me* thunders out of the huge amplifiers and all the pre-show nervousness has vanished. Morten lip-syncs so convincingly that he almost believes himself that he's actually singing. Pal hammers on the guitar so fiercely that blood spurts from his skinny fingers, and Mags sways and attacks the keyboards in perfect time with the music. Naturally the camera focusses on all three handsome faces, and both the producer of the show and the manager of the group are all smiles. The moment of truth! Everyone is satisfied.

That evening a white limousine whisks us to Paul Young's concert. In the darkness we can sneak in unobserved, but in the interval it's impossible for us to deny that, yes, it *is* actually *a*-h*a* sitting here, in the flesh, amongst the audience. Suddenly there's complete confusion as autographs, hugs and kisses are demanded once more. Morten happily signs bits of paper, while Mags pulls his jacket up over his head and hides!

The post-concert party is more relaxed – here it's *a*-h*a* who are the newcomers. At the table beside us sit Paul King and his band, there's Dionne Warwick and her friends and in the middle Paul Young. And later in the evening . . . yes it is! Elton John, with his customary hat and glasses, and full of charm.

We sit and discuss, slightly nervously, whether *a*-h*a* dare ask Dionne Warwick for a photograph together with them. "I don't know if she'd like

that," muses Pal. At the moment Dionne appears at our table and asks politely if *a-ha* would possibly be kind enough to join her in a picture, and could she please have their autographs? The ice is broken. Soon we're conversing with Elton John and Paul Young with the greatest of ease.

The New Faces meet Old Hands, Dionne Warwick and Elton John

Manager Terry Slater is tough. Long before there is even the remotest possibility of *a-ha* over doing it, he insists that the boys have had enough partying. As Pal and Morten depart, they are followed by mournful glances from the girls. Had they perhaps hoped for another, and different, conclusion to the evening? "Too bad we've had such a moral upbringing," jokes Morten.

Actually the boys prefer a peaceful end to the evening to living it up with the jet-set. Well, maybe 'peaceful' isn't really the description after all. Their

Elton John and Paul Young talk profiles while Morten boogies on down!

Morten sings his heart out during one of their first American TV appearances

boundless energy and the excitement of everything that is happening to them means that, despite their good intentions and an exhausting schedule, getting to sleep early is not as easy as it should be!

Thursday dawns. Another TV show. This time it's American Bandstand, one of the most popular networked programmes. And not only do I have permission to be present, but even our photographer is allowed on the set. The only condition is that he must promise not to take any pictures of Dick Clark, the presenter, before he has his make-up on. We sneak carefully into the studio and sit among the audience and TV crew. The lights are dimmed and abruptly a figure strides onto the stage. "Hi, this is Dick Clark greeting you from America's most popular TV programme, American Bandstand. Today we've got lots of exciting acts for you. The finals in the dance competition for which five hundred thousand of you viewers have sent in your votes and chosen the winners. We'll be showing a video with the phenomenal Madonna, and for the first time ever, we can present a Norwegian pop group who have taken the world by storm! From far away in the North, direct to Los Angeles, ladies and gentlemen: *a-ha* with their number one single in LA, *Take on Me*! But first, a word from our sponsors . . . "

Dick Clark, an institution on American TV, brushes a hair off his shoulder and requests more action from the hundred fresh-faced, fashionably dressed kids carousing wildly on the dance floor. The dancers create the traditional framework around the different sets in the TV show American Bandstand. The programme has actually been running for 32 years (with Dick Clark as host since the beginning) and has a viewing audience of 25 million people all over the USA.

Out in the dressing-room, or should I say apartment, complete with living room, TV, shower and bath, Mags, Pal and Morten are sitting tensely. Did I say sitting? They're in constant motion! Mags is juggling with some fruit. Morten tries on different jackets and checks his hairdo. Pal is talking on the telephone to his girlfriend in Boston. Everyone is joking and laughing. Changing the channel on the TV; watching another cartoon; flirting with the make-up girl; sticking ice-cubes down an unfortunate photographer's shirt. They play the song they're going to sing loud, LOUD on their Walkmans, get ready, hype themselves up to a superhigh pitch of excitement. But mostly they just have fun . . .

In the enormous TV studio Dick Clark is building up the excitement as he announces, "Ladies and gentlemen, the hottest act in town. Way over from Norway, *a-ha*, with the hit *Take on Me*!" Morten, Mags and Pal rush in through the crowd, grab their instruments, and the song thunders out into the huge studio.

The TV camera pans the whole studio – high up under the ceiling, out on the dance floor on rotating cranes, from left to right. With perfect precision they focus onto Mags' fingers on the keyboards, Pal posing with the guitar, and above all, Morten's face in close-up. Morten has a strong, expressive face and this, combined with his blue jeans and leather jacket image has caused the American Press to compare him with James Dean. The studio audience stare fascinated at the TV screen's close-ups.

The last chords fade away. Dick Clark weaves his way through the mass of bodies and asks the question that *a-ha* have already answered many, many times before in TV, radio and newspaper interviews. "How is it possible for a Norwegian pop group to make it big in the USA? Do you ever sing in Norwegian? Where did you get the name *a-ha*?" The boys answer professionally and routinely. Pal starts off by speaking broken English with a thick Norwegian accent, then laughs and switches over to perfect English: "I think Mags should answer that question".

Twenty five million viewers learn that *a-ha* went to England and signed a record contract, that they sing in English because they have always intended to have an international career, and that *a-ha* is a good name because it means the same thing all over the world. Dick Clark is amazed and impressed by their excellent English, and charmed by their winning smiles and ready wit. But now it's time for more music: *Train Of Thought*, also from their first album, *Hunting High And Low*. "We've never done this one on TV before," says Mags in the dressing-room before the show. "We practised twice in the hotel room yesterday evening. But that's typical – we always take things as they come. Here we are appearing on one of the USA's biggest TV shows, with hardly any practice!"

Of course it's a huge success. The audience are unanimous in their approval, applauding and screaming and *a-ha* have to practically force their way back to the dressing-room.

"How were we? Was it professional enough? Too stiff? How did my face look on TV? Did they like the jokes? Was the sound good?" Lots of questions to ease the tension. "Take it easy. I'm satisfied. And this TV show is going to sell a lot of records," answers manager Terry Slater. The

25 million people saw a-ha's appearance on Dick Clark's networked TV Show American Bandstand

boys relax. It was a good ten-minute performance – longer than Madonna's slot – on one of the USA's most popular TV programmes. The boys round off the day on a high!

Especially Pal. After all, it's his birthday today! Back at the hotel waits a big guitar-shaped birthday cake and presents. Mags decides to tease him a bit, and gives him a beautifully wrapped parcel of . . . 'men's' magazines! These are supposed to help Pal overcome his misery at being parted from his girlfriend Lauren! At last it's time to open the champagne, kindly provided by the hotel. But now we're on the move again! This time, to mix a little business with pleasure. *a-ha* have never performed live on stage together and as their first tour in the Autumn of 1986 is going to attract huge crowds, they've decided to see as many artists in concert as possible before then.

But this evening they don't want to be part of any official set-up. They'd rather ask a couple of Warner Brothers' secretaries to join them for a night out on the town. So we all crowd into two tiny VW beetles and cruise down the highway in Los Angeles.

We're on our way to a concert with the young, up-and-coming group Lone Justice. But even though the boys want to be out on their own tonight, Warner Brothers have taken the trouble to reserve seats in a little balcony overlooking the main floor of the club, with a special view of the stage.

But the earthy blues-rock of Lone Justice isn't enough!

At 2.00 am we're on our way to a concert with the Elvis-inspired rock 'n' roller Chris Isaac. The high spirits of the boys are still in evidence as Mags contrives to turn a somersault from the back seat to the front seat of the little VW filled with eight people!

The next day it's back to the grinding tour schedule and we're beginning to realise that the USA is actually a lot more than just Los Angeles. Every state, every big city, has its own target audience requiring individual marketing strategies. But obviously having made it in New York and Los Angeles is a great help, these two cities having the biggest influence on the music scene.

Concentrating on Los Angeles and New York was, therefore, a primary goal for *a-ha* at that point. Before they arrived in New York they made a quick detour to Miami, where their record company, Warner Brothers, had a sales conference. Hundreds of salesmen from all over the USA met to be presented with new artists and 'product' – the product being, of course, albums. This time *a-ha* were the guests of honour. Yet another indication that the record company really believes in our boys. For hours, Morten, Mags and Pal walked around meeting the people responsible for selling records to the record stores. And the boys proved to be experts here, too.

VW Beetle-mania! a-ha *pack 'em in.*

They conversed just as pleasantly and openly with the salesmen and businessmen as they do with their fans on the street. To top it all off, that week Warner Brothers placed a series of impressive ads in the music business bible, Billboard. On page one there were three pictures of *a*-h*a* showing the group and the record company thanking all the representatives at the Miami meeting for their efforts so far, with *a*-h*a* gracing the centre-spread in the form of a large poster.

The record company meeting in Miami had to be content with this one-day visit, as the boys had to take the 'red-eye', or night plane, to gain some time. Now they were ready to take a bite out of the Big Apple – New York City!

Here the PR machinery was going full force again. Terry Slater continued to pick and choose wisely. Only the biggest teen magazines and the most prestigious publications like Andy Warhol's Interview and the grand-daddy of them all, Rolling Stone, could count on getting close to them.

a-h*a* were so well-known that both they and their manager Terry Slater booked themselves into the Berkshire Palace Hotel under assumed names, to avoid telephone calls and other unnecessary disturbances.

The following week the music-TV station MTV was to present their yearly video prizes, and the city was full of pop stars. Sheila E, Julian Lennon and Wham! were staying at our hotel. The fans who waited all day and night outside the entrance and in the lobby now recognised *a*-h*a* immediately. So every time they went in or out of the hotel they were mobbed by hoards of autograph and photo hunters.

It wasn't all work though, and we got invited to a number of parties. Sitting in the back seat of yet another long limousine on the way to a reception Mags checks whether his accidental discovery made during one of the first limousine trips in Los Angeles is the same all over the USA. What happened was that when he tried to turn on the apparently old-fashioned radio in the backseat of the long car, what flooded out was not music, but scotch! He tried another station – vodka. Yet another – gin. So he concluded that all proper limousines are equipped with their own hidden bars.

The party this evening is for David Lee Roth who is leaving Van Halen, and is being held at the trendy Palladium. This turns out to be much bigger than the private parties we attended in Los Angeles. The Palladium holds thousands of people – and it is jam-packed! But *a*-h*a* not only manage to slip in ahead of the long queue waiting outside, but are also able to get through the rope closures blocking the VIP area, where Morten and I seek refuge after nearly being trampled to death at the bar. We immediately catch sight of the lovely Brooke Shields clinging rather intimately to George Michael of Wham! "They make an attractive couple, but I don't think there's much future there," remarks Morten who can't wait to get out of the

a-ha 'down under' at the Sydney Opera House

place and go home.

Home now means a hotel room for *a-ha*. Only a few months ago they had to drape plastic over their heads to avoid rain leaking from the ceiling of John Ratcliff's dilapidated studio in London. Now they're living in a $200 a day suite in New York. But they'll only be there for a few days because Morten has promised to attend his elder brother's wedding in Oslo. Mags wants to set up an apartment with Heidi, and Pal is going to Boston to see Lauren.

After catching up with family and personal affairs, they're back together in London again for more PR interviews and more meetings, but primarily to start production for their video for *The Sun Always Shines on TV*. On arrival in London they receive the news that *Take on Me* has gone all the way to the top of the Billboard chart in the USA. Number One! On Friday, October 11, three proud boys board the plane to Australia. But it's a long, long way to the other side of the earth – the trip takes 27 hours! The jet lag after the trip to Los Angeles is nothing compared to this.

On arrival in Sydney, the local record company representative immediately offers to take us sight-seeing. Morten, Mags and I accept. But

The Production Assistant restrains an over enthusiastic cameraman during a TV interview in Australia

it's not only raining, it's pouring! All our hopes of sun, summer, surfing and swimming are soon dampened by the down-pour. But we get to see Sydney anyway – in yet another long limousine, without a bar for once. We see the storm-soaked beaches on the outskirts of the city; the Opera House with its unusual architectural design; the harbour full of restaurants and, of course, Sydney Harbour Bridge.

Manager Terry Slater follows his usual routine: a few days off before the serious business begins.

After our first day in Australia, we all felt the jet-lag creep up on us in one way or another. Pal went out to play snooker in the middle of the night, Mags ate dinner at breakfast-time and I went for 48 hours without sleep.

But *a-ha* were soon back to work. More TV shows, more interviews, more photo sessions. Work, work, work. The only difference was that the

"Captain" Mags salutes the world

journalists here asked what the boys thought of Australia, instead of Los Angeles.

We manage to find time for a boat trip . . . in the middle of a storm. We can't do any shark-fishing, but we do get to see some real waves. The ocean spray drenches the whole boat, and we all get soaked, but even amidst the 30 foot waves the three members of *a*-h*a* and their manager thoroughly enjoy themselves.

Mags and Morten, in particular, are having great fun clowning around for the benefit of the photographers present. Mags hangs from the side of the boat and gives them all a 'Captain's' salute, while Morten, with his brand new camera, tries to snap the photographers snapping him! However, Pal is getting rather fed up with the whole thing – and is heard to curse loudly when one of the photographers, with profuse apologies, tells them that the roll of film showing the boys in front of the Opera House has been swept overboard . . . and would they mind terribly doing it all again? But, ever the professionals, they all trudge back out into the rain once more.

Eventually they return to the hotel to be greeted with sunnier news. *Take on Me* is soaring up the charts in England, Canada, Japan, Sweden, Germany . . . you name it. Mags has a favourite quotation from one of the Doors' songs, "We want the world and we want it now." For *a*-h*a* these are no longer just words because they are conquering the world! So the tour continues . . . and new challenges await.

Manager Terry Slater
in the picture for once

Morten asks
'What me pose for a picture?'

Pal 'fishing
for a line

Up and . . .

Over

and Down Under

Mags showing off his diving prowess.

The Sun Always Shines on Pal

a-h

a-ha
hunting high and low

*Morten loves
New York City*

SONOR

Morten Harket

Pal on Morten:
"Morten is totally different from me. When we first came to London together, he burned all my clothes and re-dressed me from head to toe. I don't care much about clothes, whereas he's always very interested in them. He has given me self-confidence, encourages me to talk to people, not to be afraid and to use the abilities I have.

Morten is actually the only one in Norway who had as much ambition as I did. I guess we both have big egos. In a way we're each sitting in our own little world, while Mags is more down to earth. Mags often has to mediate between Morten and me . . . It's good that we're so different and still respect each other. The tension between us is creative. No one sings like Morten. He's got what it takes and I have great faith in him."

Mags on Morten:
"What's nice about Morten is that he's so together. He believes strongly in everything he does. This goes for the band too, and it rubs off on us. He has the courage of his own convictions and cannot be shaken. He's an expert at always getting the last word, whether he's right or not. Morten is very loyal and he's fair when it comes to giving people a chance, letting them show who they are and what they're worth before judging them."

Morten on himself:
"I flirt a bit too much with too many things, I guess. My self-discipline is terrible when it comes to working. I always have great visions of music and other things which I can see the outlines of, but which I don't get around to doing anything about. I guess I'm really a dreamer."

Morten Harket was born on 14 September 1959 in the town of Kongsberg. He was number two in a family of five children, four boys and one girl. His father, Reidar, is now chief physician at a hospital. His mother, Henny, is a recently qualified Home Economics teacher.

Morten has a great need for emotional security, as his childhood and school years were not exactly easy for him. He was unusually self-confident from an early age, often disappearing from home and running around on his own which would frighten his poor mother out of her wits. Morten built up a fantasy world which could often seem more real to him than the real world.

"Starting school was a total disaster for me," says Morten. "It's always been easy for me to let my thoughts wander freely, and they seldom come back down to earth. I couldn't differentiate between fantasy and reality. It didn't matter to me if a story I told was true or something I made up.

"I was constantly getting beaten up. Just about every day. The third, fourth and fifth grades were the worst. It was awful. Luckily I had a pretty long walk home from school so I had enough time to calm down a bit before I got back. But sometimes I'd arrive home in a real mess, with tears still running down my cheeks."

Morten lived in another world at home which had little or nothing to do with school. But he felt most comfortable in his third 'world', his imagination. He could bring this to life not only by making up stories, but also through his drawing, at which he had become very proficient.

In his dreams he was always strong and powerful . . . the leader. One he remembers in particular is where he is riding into school on a white horse, followed by his teacher (with whom he was head over heels in love) also on a white horse. Two black panthers accompany him, pulling an aquarium on wheels containing a shark . . . however, he can't remember how the dream ended!

But in reality: "Those were tough years. It has always been a mystery to me how I survived it all the way I did. It could have messed me up but, in fact, it has made me stronger. It has given me a total lack of respect for mobs, cliques and narrow-minded people who don't think for themselves. I feel that it's healthy to go against the mainstream of public opinion", says Morten.

The elementary school years were the worst, and it went on in secondary school, too, to some extent. But at that point, Morten joined the Christian Union.

In the Union, Morten made new friends, friends who knew nothing of his past problems – and he was given a fresh chance. They listened to his stories attentively and laughed good-naturedly at him and with him. When it came to light that he was unusually good at drawing, he rose even higher in the estimation of his new friends. This positive encouragement made him want to use his drawing ability more constructively, not just as a means of private escape. Morten gradually became a central figure within his circle, a kind of leader, and as a result his self-confidence blossomed once again.

Morten had a religious experience at this time, which was to have a profound effect on the rest of his life. Morten's parents are active members of the church, and until then religion had been something he had grown up with and taken for granted. Now he was able to make up his own mind about his belief:

"You can't fool yourself when it comes to matters like this. It's all about honesty. The certainty that something is greater than yourself, and that that something is Love, makes submission easy. I know it's good for me to learn that kind of obediance. It gives me a feeling of safety and belonging," says Morten.

After Heggedel Elementary School and Solvent Secondary School, Morten made his way to Asker Gymnasium, an upper secondary school which prepares students for university. There was nothing wrong with his natural aptitude towards learning and Morten's grades were basically fairly good, but his concentration was poor and his head full of other things. So, he was somewhat surprised when he received the highest grade in Christianity. He made a sudden decision to begin studying at the Theological Seminary. Apart from his very real interest in the Bible, he was attracted by the 'minister' image. He would don the robes of the clergy, have really long hair . . . but then there was also his interest in music . . .

Morten's love of music started at the tender age of three when he was taken to see a local marching band. His sensitive temperament was immediately attracted to the emotional music, and he started crying and laughing and got into the spirit of the music to such an extent that the band leader noticed him and lifted him up onto his shoulders to conduct the band. The youngster was thrilled.

Morten's father is musically talented and had difficulty choosing between a career as a classical pianist or a doctor. Morten took piano lessons as a boy, but it was too strict a discipline for him. He practised very little and didn't learn to read music. But he did compose and liked to improvise on the instrument for his own pleasure.

Morten managed to exist happily in total ignorance of pop music, until the summer before he was to begin at the Gymnasium. Then Jimi Hendrix and Uriah Heep changed his life.

"At the time I collected butterflies and cultivated orchids. I was totally absorbed by that. Then I got a complete collection of Uriah Heep LPs, and there was only one group in the world for me. It was at this time I really started to enjoy my music. I could hear exactly what I wanted to do inside me and when I sang, I could go for hours without knowing where I was. It was incredible. I'm sure that it beats any kind of chemical trip. Only the feeling of being in love or tremendously infatuated can be as strong as this."

But one day he woke up and realised that he had nothing to show for it. He had dreams and ambitions. But results . . .? The period when he sang in the professional band Souldier Blue was a breakthrough for Morten. Finally he had managed to channel his creativity.

"Arild was the boss in Souldier Blue, I was just the vocalist. But I learnt a lot about singing and about being in a band and by February 1982, after only two months of rehearsing, I was on stage singing in front of an audience. I don't remember anything about the performance except that I was scared stiff. A few electric seconds, minutes or hours passed, and some guy came over and stuffed £60 in my pocket. I actually earned money singing!"

On the surface it looked as though everything was beginning to fall into place for Morten. He was studying theology, had completed his military service, and had an outlet for his creative ability in singing and performing with Souldier Blue. He still lived at home with his parents but he was considering taking a small flat in Oslo. Morten appeared to be establishing himself, but a bet he made with one of his fellow students betrayed his restlessness. He knew that one day he was going to become a rock star.

Just then, Mags called him up and asked if he would like to join him in a new band . . .

Mags Furuholmen

Morten on Mags:
"Mags is ingeniously childish and childishly ingenious. He is talented, spontaneous and impulsive. He does everything recklessly and with so much energy. In contrast to Pal, Mags is totally disorganised and has no self discipline at all. Of the three of us, he is the one who really knows how to live life to the full. Everything happens around Mags. Personally, I've learned an awful lot from being around him."

Pal on Mags:
"Mags is impulsive. Dashes around. Throughout the years I've often wondered: Is he a complete fool or a genius? Has he got talent or hasn't he? He can say things which are really dumb, but then he'll suddenly switch on, put things in their place and come up with the idea that we've all been fumbling for. I think he's both a fool and a genius. There has, at times, been a tough competitive relationship between us, which has been a driving force for us both. I have always had great respect for him and belief in him as an artist and musician."

Mags on himself:
"I have always been hyperactive. I've always been told that I waste too much energy on the wrong things, but I think it's better to do everything and rely on some of it being worthwhile."

Magne (Mags) Furuholmen was born on 1 November 1962. His mother is a teacher and his father was a musician. The family lived at Manglerud, a predominantly working class area in Oslo. Mags' father, Kare Furuholmen, played the trumpet in a dance band called Bent Solve's Orchestra. When Mags was only five years old, the plane the band was travelling in crashed just outside Oslo, and his father was killed. His mother, Annelise, remarried after a while, and Mags now has one sister and two brothers. "My father had a great deal of musical ambition although he never got a chance to carry it out. However, it seems to be alive in me because I became so absorbed in music at an early age. To some extent it took priority over things like school, private life and everything else," says Mags in retrospect. "I'm not doing what I'm doing today for my father's sake. I'm doing it for my own sake, but I know that it means a lot to the people in my family if you try to achieve the goals you have set for yourself."

His mother and grandfather have both given their undivided support to Mags' efforts to probe the mysteries of music. They know that it was in the family. In spite of the tragic loss of his father at such an early age, Mags feels that he had a happy and secure childhood. He always got along well with his stepfather, and is very close to his mother. He met Pal when he was ten, and they quickly became good friends. Their common interest in music did not really manifest itself until Mags was in the seventh grade. It was then that he began to listen to people like Janis Joplin, Jimi Hendrix and the Doors. The total involvement of these artists with their music became a challenge to Mags and he was no longer able to treat his own music as just an amusement. He had to make a choice, and he chose to go into music, even though it meant distancing himself from his friends. Jim Morrison and Jimi Hendrix didn't quite fit into the classroom or the flats at Manglerud. Mags became an outsider. He let his hair grow and became a hippy at a time when it wasn't 'in' to be one. When he was fifteen years old, the family moved to Asker, a fairly well-to-do suburb of Oslo. This was a real culture shock for Mags. "I was an avowed anarchist at that time and expected to find spoilt kids with rich parents. And I found them, of course. My freaky appearance, long hair and taste in music were pretty unusual – I was considered a weirdo. But I was never made fun of or bullied. It was actually the time I spent at the Gymnasium in Asker which changed my personality. I learned to be more tolerant of people who were different from me, and in turn I found they became more tolerant of me. Most of the friends I have today are from that period at the Gymnasium." He was an average student at school - there were other things in life more important than homework. School became an obligation to fulfil in order to satisfy parents and teachers. Mags completed his degree at the Gymnasium, even though he really wanted to go to London with Pal long before he finished school. But it was not only school that kept Mags from going. There was Heidi, the Girl in his life.

Mags positively bursts with energy. He's the one who might jostle you in fun, who will challenge you to a race, who dives and windsurfs, who is physically active. He's also a great fan of electronic games, like Space

Invaders, which he can play for hours at a time – always managing to end up with the highest score!

But behind the loud, extrovert personality lies a searching soul. Mags spends a lot of time by himself thinking, and is very concerned about the misuse of power. He refused to do his military service and so, was given 'conscientious objector' status.

"There are many ideologies which attempt to explain everything, to put things into place once and for all. I look at the Christian religion as one of several ideologies. The Bible stems from a true understanding of what a group of people need in order to live together. There is a great deal of wisdom in it, but I think it represents a system created by a minority to regulate the affairs of other people. I don't believe in all-encompassing solutions. I like to look around with an open mind. Leave room for change and development. I think that greed for power is one of the major forces motivating peoples lives, and that it so easily becomes power in the sense of oppression of others. That's misuse of power. I think that power in the sense of developing your inner resources is important. The feeling of really mastering something, and using your ability to the full.

"Precisely because we are such individualists, driven by a desire for power, it is extremely important to cultivate solidarity and loyalty towards one another. We all share responsibility for the society we live in. I hate political extremism, dogmatic beliefs and the cultivation of an elite; the idea that some know better than others and therefore have the right to control them. It's fine to be an individual and not want to follow the crowd but it is dangerous to start thinking that your ideas are the only ones that count -and to try and force your ideas on others." he says.

Mags, like Pal and Morten, was very interested in drawing at one time. A friend of his, who is now attending the National College of Arts, Crafts and Design in Oslo, was the first person Mags met who had a burning, creative desire - he knew he was going to be a painter. Mags was inspired by him and began to draw himself; rather grotesque, abstract drawings. After a while music took over as the outlet for his creative urge. He was, however, on the verge of beginning at an art school in London during a stagnant period in *a-ha*'s development.

Mags' family accepted his total absorbtion in music. When they moved to Oslo they had more room in the house, and Pal and Mags were allowed to move into the basement with their instruments and sound equipment. They practised for several hours at a stretch, five or six times a week. They divided the instruments between them. Both played guitar and keyboards and Pal continued to play the drums. They became so accustomed to playing together that, after a while, they could communicate without words. Pal would play two notes, and Mags would continue perfectly naturally with the next ten.

Pal has done most of the composing until now. But Mags has made a conscious effort to pull together his ideas and get them down on paper or onto a tape and the second *a-ha* LP will probably contain quite a few of his compositions.

Pal Waaktaar

Morten on Pal:
"Pal has unbelievable self-discipline and is a workaholic. He can keep working on what appears to be the same thing over and over again. While I go crazy when I have to go over a song hundreds of times, he can sit with it for hours, trying to find exactly the right mix to achieve the sound he wants. Pal is really the driving force behind *a-ha*. He's one of the few real artists on the pop-rock scene. It's always exciting to hear what he's written."

Mags on Pal:
"Pal is the person who has meant most to me in my musical development, and yet he's the one person who I find it most difficult to say anything sensible about. He has incredible will-power and a watchful eye which is always searching for material he can use creatively. In a way I have idolized Pal for years, and I still depend on him to help me sort out my own ideas."

Pal on himself:
"I like to keep in the background. There are only certain kinds of people I can talk to, feel secure with. In any case, I'm certainly not the pop-star type. I lack some of the characteristics necessary in this business, like enjoying PR stunts. What's important to me is creativity, musical ambitions; I'm afraid of mediocrity."

Pal Gamst Waaktaar was born on September 6, 1961. His family moved from Tonsenhagen to Manglerud when he was one year old. He has one sister, Tonge, who is two years older than him. His father is a pharmacist, and his mother works for the telephone company. Both parents are very interested in classical music, and regularly took Pal to concerts, operas and the ballet when he was young.

Pal describes his childhood and youth as relatively normal. He was slightly better than average at school, but never managed to work up much enthusiasm for schoolwork. Early in life his interests began to develop in other directions, with music already taking an important role. When Pal began to play the recorder as a child, he immediately started composing his own melodies. He also loved drawing and was content to sit by himself for hours and pursue his own interests.

He didn't like Manglerud School, and switched to Nordstrand, the very last all-boys' school in Norway.

"It was around that time that the sixties hit me. I wore wide bellbottoms, grew my hair long and hung up Jimi Hendrix posters. At Nordstrand the boys were all clean, crew-cut kids driving around in their rich fathers' cars. Everybody else's style was completely alien to me, and I had no desire to become like them. I've always wanted to be different," he recalls.

Drawing took up much of his time, but by the age of ten, Pal was composing tunes for poems, some of which he still remembers to this day. Then he heard the record of the musical 'Hair'. He listened to it repeatedly and began to dream about playing keyboards to his own music. Instead he ended up building his own set of drums and playing along to records. His friend Mags joined in and inspired by 'Hair' they decided to write their own rock opera.

Pal had girl problems, too. He was convinced that he would die a virgin! He would always fall for the unattainable ones. When he was thirteen, a girl developed a crush on him, and she had ten of her friends take turns visiting Pal at home, every day for three weeks. He was scared to death and took to staying away from home all day to avoid having to answer the doorbell. Pal was eighteen years old when he finally got his first kiss, and that was from Mags' girlfriend. She was looking for revenge after an argument and so, to make Mags jealous, she kissed Pal right in front of him. But the romance with Pal only lasted three days, before she went back to Mags. After that experience Pal became even more frightened of rejection and gave up completely . . . for the time being!

In high school Pal was the typical 'aspiring artist' — sitting at the back of the classroom with his thoughts miles away. He barely graduated due to poor attendance, and Pal's teachers nicknamed him 'The Guest'.

He preferred to stay at home and make music with Mags. By this time they had progressed to electric guitars and keyboard instruments. As their music became more and more advanced, so their friendship grew. They worked well together, but the friendship wasn't perfect by any means — it was characterised by keen competition between the two. One summer they travelled through Europe and at one point they stopped speaking to each other communicating solely through song lyrics they wrote! But despite the quarrels their music kept them together — even after Mags' family moved to Asker.

The house at Asker had more room for them to practise in, and Pal was up there almost every day — or at least every weekend. Pal's music reflected his moods. He wrote all the lyrics for the Bridges album and everything centred on one subject: his frustration in love!

"That album is actually about my first real kiss, about how at last I felt like a member of the human race. About how relieved and happy I was that it had happened — that someone wanted to be with me. About how I had grown up to the extent that I had thought it was rotten to be alone and about my disappointment when I realised how little she really was involved, but how something in me had been awakened anyway," says Pal.

Before they were in their teens Pal and Mags decided they would have to go to England to get their big break. They were convinced that they would be as famous as the Beatles! Pal wanted to leave for London as soon as he had graduated, but as he was a year older than Mags, he had to wait one more year.

Pal didn't really do much except wait for Mags to graduate. Like Mags, Pal was a conscientious objector and so didn't do military service, but during that year Pal discovered literature. Having felt nothing for literature in school, Pal suddenly realised what he had been missing – books! He was fascinated, and bought all the Penguin Classics he could get his hands on, English paperbacks being cheaper than Norwegian translations. He spent days sitting in Oslo cafes with his books.

Reading was only interrupted by writing new song lyrics and during this time he became greatly influenced by the Doors. Their music was powerful but their lyrics were even more so. They were personal and direct. That was how he wanted *his* lyrics to sound.

Pal's notebook is his most important working tool. It accompanies him everywhere, day and night. It's here that he sketches and records impressions, overheard conversations, interesting words from the TV, ideas and observations. A song lyric can start life as a few words on page 3, develop a refrain on page 15, be revised on page 33, and finished in book number 3, page 12.

"It has become a way of life," explains Pal. "When you talk to people, you have to remember that any little snippet can turn into a song. So you sit there ready to steal the one line that shines out. It's the same when you read books, see films, or write letters."

He goes on: "When I write lyrics in English, I feel it's an advantage to be Norwegian, because I see the language as something exciting and full of possibilities. I can pick out ordinary words or phrases and make them sound new and interesting. For example, I can write songs like *Hunting High and Low* or *Train Of Thought*, and English people will comment on their interesting or unusual titles, even though they are phrases that they themselves use all the time. Look at *Take On Me*. Most people have to think twice about the title before they get to like it. To me, to 'take on' somebody means to notice them and take time to find out what they're really like. *Take On Me* almost becomes 'Look! Here I am!'"

The most recent inspiration for Pal's lyrics has come from his relationship with Lauren, an American girl he met in London in the early days. Once more he could pour his emotions into his songs.

"My contributions to the album *Hunting High and Low* are about really being in love for the first time in my life. They're very romantic, but also realistic. I live in England, she lives in America, so there's always this underlying fear that it can never last. I mean, months can go by without our being able to meet. All the songs on the album were written in an attempt to secure a place in her heart for me. I wanted to put so much of myself into her that she couldn't live without me. I admit I used every musical trick in the book to get her to love me. Every single song is a prayer for attention . . . Take On Me!"

SONOR

The Music

a-h*a* are musically ambitious. Ever since they began writing music as teenagers, they have had high aspirations. Pal and Mags wanted to write a rock opera. Morten felt that music had the power to change people.

Classical music has been a subconscious source of inspiration for them. However, the boys have drawn their main inspiration from such musical giants of the rock world as the Doors and Jimi Hendrix, with their raw and uncompromising music, as well as from the simple but catchy tunes for which the Beatles are still the best example.

Up till now we only have one album, *Hunting High and Low*, to judge them by, so it is still too early to know whether *a*-h*a*'s musical ambitions will be realised. The Bridges album appeared too early in their development, and the trial demo tapes of songs that weren't included on *Hunting High and Low* have still to be released. However, their first album already sees them exhibiting an impressive range of material. *Take On Me* is an optimistic pop song with an unusually catchy intro. The keyboard theme is constructed with ingenious simplicity, and the melody gives Morten the opportunity to exploit his full vocal range. The song also demonstrates one of *a*-h*a*'s greatest assets; the combination of Morten's strong, clear voice, together with their complex, powerful musical accompaniment. Morten has a unique voice. He can sing a melody alone, but is also capable, like Freddy Mercury of Queen, of producing a whole choir of voices by himself.

The second song on the album, *Train Of Thought*, reveals the group's other side: Morten's voice pitched in an even, deep range, with an almost exaggerated dramatic expression, while sombre background harmonies create a gloomy atmosphere. Added to this we get the purposefully monotonous bass-synth and rhythm that hold it all together.

The Sun Always Shines On TV and *Hunting High and Low* display the group at their most symphonic. The first contains some dramatic mood alterations. A quiet, almost religious opening with piano, Morten's high voice and the floating synth-harmonies builds up to a crescendo that explodes into a guitar riff that any heavy metal band would envy. But the riff is only repeated a few times, then the music takes off in other directions. It isn't until later in the song that Morten introduces the main melody line which culminates in the powerful refrain. The different ingredients shift throughout the song – once again with effective use of pauses and rests. I think it's the strongest hit single on the whole album and it says a lot about *a*-h*a*'s potential.

Hunting High and Low is quieter, almost a ballad, with a lonely acoustic guitar in the introduction backing up Morten's clear voice. Seagull cries, piano, synth-strings and overdubbing of Morten's different vocals build up towards a short section where horns (synthesizers here too) rise into an almost baroque theme. The melodic development is unusual for a ballad as it's not tied to one key theme, but changes from mood to mood.

The Blue Sky seems to be a more traditional, ordinary synth-pop song where the main impression is created by the bubbling drum machines and synth-bass. *Love is Reason* has some of the same artificiality, but is saved by a very effective refrain which offsets the mechanical precision in the accompaniment.

Living A Boy's Adventure Tale attempts some of the same symphonic effects as *The Sun Always Shines On TV* but doesn't quite take off to the same degree. Although a synth-oboe gives fine contrast to Morten's voice and the melody is powerful, the arrangement is not quite as creative and effective.

And You Tell Me might have been inspired by the natural exuberance the Beatles displayed in their prime. It is light and airy, without a strong underlying rhythm, but it has delicate harmonies coupled with surprising synthesiser effects which unexpectedly dominate the tune.

The music on the album *Hunting High and Low* demonstrates a group with its finger on the musical pulse of the eighties. All the positive elements of the synth-pop movement are present and there's a full appreciation for the commercial pop-refrain. Fortunately this is enhanced by musical themes and chord changes that raise it beyond the simple pop framework. Thus the music acquires a much longer life-span – it tolerates continual listening. You can come back to it again and again.

It is, as yet, too soon to know whether *a*-h*a* will accomplish their ultimate goal and become musical legends. But they've made a more than promising beginning with a first album that has shown they are far from being a 'one hit wonder'.

The Lyrics

Pal studies his notebook which has been the inspiration behind every a-ha song.

THE BLUE SKY

I find it hard to breathe
As life just eats away
At the faces that surround me
They look tired today
The lady at my table
Doesn't want me here
I just want to talk to her
But would she laugh at my accent
And make fun of me
It doesn't seem like
This blue sky's here for me

There are no girls in here
As far as I can see
Only pin-up posters
Looking down at me
Watching papercups of coffee
Growing cold before my eyes
All the things I see
That make me realize
I'm in this big world without you
Nothing to my name
I never knew
That blue sky meant such pain

I'm dying to be different
In the coffee shop
I lived at double strength
Now my supplies are cut
Oh, I'm older than my looks
And older than my years
I'm too young to take on
My deepest fears
I used to be confused
But now I just don't know
Since you left I've been watching
Blue skies come and go

TRAIN OF THOUGHT

He likes to have
The morning paper crossword solved
Words go up, words come down
Forwards, backwards, twisted round
He grabs a pile of letters
From a small suitcase
Disappears into an office
It's another working day

And his thoughts
Are full of strangers
Corridors of naked light
And his mind
Once full of reason
Now there's more that meets the eye
Now a stranger's face
He carries with him

He likes a bit of reading
On the subway home
A distant radio whistling tunes
That nobody knows
At home a house awaits him
He unlocks the door
Thinking once there was a sea here
But there never was a door

And his thoughts
Are full of strangers
And his eyes too numb to see
And nothing that he knows of
And nowhere where he's been
Was ever quite like this

And the heart is full of strangers
Dodging on his train of thought
Train of thought

THE SUN ALWAYS SHINES ON TV

Touch me
How can it be
Believe me
The sun always shines on TV
Hold me
Close to your heart
Touch me
And give all your love to me

I reached inside myself and found
Nothing there to ease the pressure
Off my ever worrying mind
All my powers waste away
I fear the crazy lonely looks
The mirror's sending me these days

Please don't ask me to defend
The shameful lowlands of the way
I'm drifting gloomingly through time
I reached inside myself today
Thinkin' there's got to be some way
To keep my troubles distant

Hold me
Close to your heart
Touch me
And give all your love to me

HUNTING HIGH AND LOW

Here I am
And within the reach of my hand
She's sound asleep
And she's sweeter now
Than the wildest dream
Could have seen her
And I watch her slipping away
Though I know I'll be

Hunting high and low
Ah, there's no end
To the lengths I'll go

Find her again
Upon this my dreams are depending
Through the dark
I sense the pounding of her heart
Next to mine
She's the sweetest love
I could find
So I guess I'll be

Hunting high and low
Do you know what it means
To love you

I'm hunting high and low
And now she's telling me
She's got to go away
Watch me tearing myself to pieces
For you I'll be hunting high and low

A-HA: "THE SUN ALWAYS SHINES ON T.V."
DIR: STEVE BARRON
CAM O. STAPLETON...
LINE:
14
TAKE
1
9TH OCT 85 // DOUBLE X 5222 //
LIMELIGHT 246.

The Videos

a-h*a*'s videos have played an important part in bringing the group to the attention of the record-buying public. It was the inspired combination of cartoon and regular film in the now 'classic' video for *Take On Me* that was the decisive factor for *a*-h*a*'s success in the USA and the rest of the world. *Take On Me* also exists in another video version, a version most of those involved would prefer to forget. During this period the boys were constantly commuting between London and Oslo, waiting for The Big Breakthrough. They were suddenly informed that a video was under production. Once on set they couldn't believe their eyes: they had their own caravan as a dressing-room, another for relaxation, and yet another as a restaurant. The studio was a dream: with all the most sophisticated and expensive photographic, lighting and sound equipment.

The initial concept was that the video should present the boys rehearsing. Eventually it was decided that there should be some girls in the audience . . . *a*-h*a* weren't too sure about that. They didn't want to be part of the 'bring on the dancing girls' attitude so prevalent in rock videos. But the powers that be had already made their decision . . .

In one scene Morten was supposed to be 'auditioning' at the microphone stand. Suddenly Mags came storming out of the restaurant van and trying to catch his breath, told Morton what had happened. He and Pal had been sitting innocently having a meal, when a group of girls, as a joke, provocatively waltzed in and began to undress. Mags and Pal tried desperately to ignore the whole thing and continued eating, when some of the naked girls started leaning over their plates. Things got even worse when Mags tried to turn around, and his face ended up in the bare behind of a girl who was bending over to pull up her net stockings! At this point Mags ran.

The boys' collective reaction was: What in the world are they trying to do to an innocent song like *Take On Me*? Apparently the record company's bright idea was to prove to all the world that *a*-h*a* were normal, red-blooded males. They didn't want them to have the sexually ambiguous image of so many of the pop groups of the time. As the filming proceeded the *a*-h*a* boys grew more and more uncertain. The ending was supposed to show a crowd of girls storming the set while *a*-h*a* escaped into a waiting limousine. A few girls were then supposed to sneak into the car, stark naked. And then *a*-h*a* were to be seen 'getting friendly' with the girls as the car drove away from the camera.

It didn't work. The boys weren't willing to put up with it. To cap it all, the video team used the identical set for a hard-core porno film with the same girls – some of whom were professional striptease dancers and mud-wrestlers – after *a*-h*a* left. Or, to be more correct, after *a*-h*a* were thrown out!

"We felt sorry for the girls," says Morten, although he too had found himself in an embarrassing situation when one of the girls purposely pulled

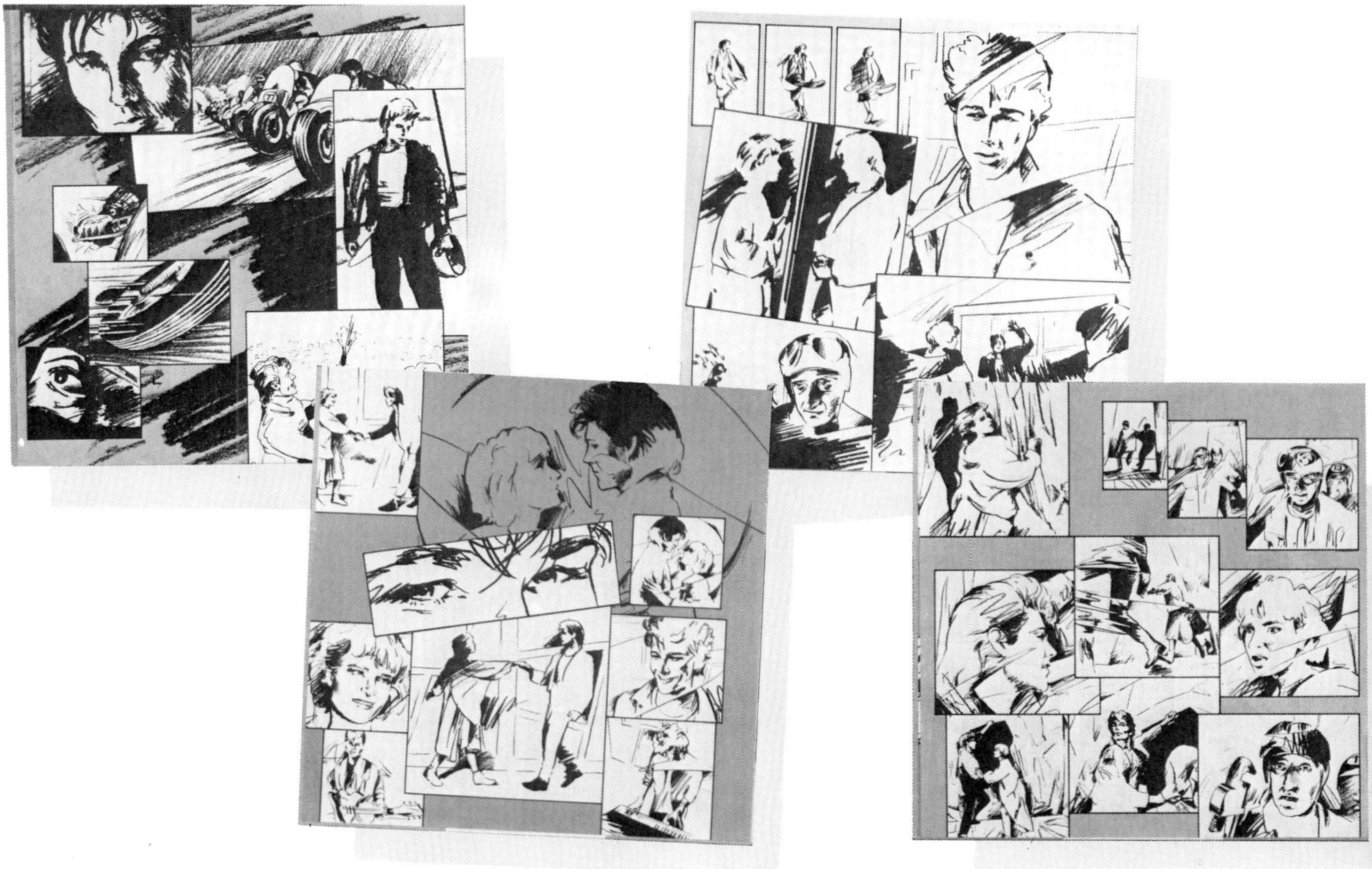

off her sweater and shoved her breasts into his face. "You see," he goes on, "a lot of the girls were hopeful seventeen year-olds who wanted to be models, and dancers who needed the money. They weren't into the heavy stuff." He shrugs it off as just a strange episode in their career. "I think someone took pictures during the filming, with naked girls holding us tightly around our chests. Mags just froze . . . he didn't know what to do with his hands! It was a terrible video – the first one – our 'Blue Movie'."

But things were to improve. Warner Brothers' Senior Vice President, Jeff Ayeroff, wanted to put his new 'blue-eyed boys' in an innovative form of video. It all came out of an old idea he had, a combination of cartoon and regular film. Michael Patterson had created a unique form of animation which could be called a work of art: 'Commuter'. In black and white, with a technique far beyond the traditional children's cartoons like Fred Flintstone and Donald Duck it contained restlessly moving figures and portrait likenesses, flickering, searching.

Ayeroff introduced Patterson to video director Steve Barron, who had developed a reputation as the best in the business after his video for Michael Jackson's *Billy Jean*. Ayeroff explained that he wanted a story about a comic strip character who comes to life and takes a girl back with him into the comic strip. "Don't be concerned about the story in the song. The song is strong enough to stand on its own. What we need is a video that can attract attention independently of the song. We have a good record – now we need a good video."

Four months and about £125,000 later, Barron and Patterson showed up with the final version of the video for *Take On Me*.

Each of the boys in *a*-h*a* has his own charm and personality, but together they form an effective visual unit. Their appearance was decisive in Ayeroff's willingness to go all the way for *a*-h*a*. They could wait to exploit the boys' natural good looks – *Take On Me* was strong enough on its own. It

Morten's no dummy when it comes to performing in the group's video

was therefore an advantage that the video was primarily in cartoon form – what did these boys really look like? When the viewers finally got to see the boys close up, no doubt was left as to their visual appeal and attraction.

In video number two, for *The Sun Always Shines On TV*, it was decided to focus more on the boys' faces. The job was again assigned to Steve Barron and his Limelight Production Company and two days were set aside for *a*-h*a* to film in London. That was enough because Steve Barron had prepared everything thoroughly. He had found the perfect location – an old vacated church, St. Albany's, just outside London. Fifty men had worked for almost a week to get it ready. High scaffolding outside the church supported enormous floodlights which lit up the whole church and cast gloomy patterns through the stained glass windows. The church itself was filled with 650 dummies of the sort you would normally find in department store windows. At one end hung a huge painting of another church, so the effect was that of an endless church hall. On the stage, instruments and microphones were set up. Around this area – behind bars, under the pulpit, between pillars – sat dummies properly clad in evening dress holding the instruments of a classical orchestra. The mobile side walls with hundreds of

Morten, Mags, video director Steve Barron, and Pal in St. Albany's Church

stone faces carved in relief didn't exactly lighten the sombre surroundings. Smoke machines intensified this atmosphere while Steve Barron guided the camera up and down, capturing the group's faces from every conceivable and inconceivable angle.

It was two days of constant filming with the boys miming the song, first separately and then as a group. The only interruptions were new rounds of make-up, some breaks for food and occasional rest periods. Again they had their own caravans for eating, sleeping, relaxing and dressing.

It was all filmed in black and white and hand-painted to achieve the special effect. Naturally it was expensive, there were no short cuts on this video. When you have a number one hit behind you, a powerful follow-up is essential.

Videos have been especially important for *a*-h*a*. It was when the final version of the video for *Take On Me* was finished that Jeff Ayeroff really knew he had a winner. The video was so sensational that Warner Brothers decided to release the video before the single. It was distributed to TV stations and shown to people in the music business for weeks before the single was released. As a result, everyone in the business in the USA was talking about *a*-h*a* before they had the remotest idea of who, or what, they were. The video itself had created the necessary 'buzz' to make people in the music industry and in the media sit up and take notice.

Terry Slater — the fourth member of a-ha

Manager Terry Slater is a vital part of the story of *a*-h*a*. His lifetime of experience in the music business has helped him to guide the group's career through all the pitfalls with a paternal hand. Well, he is old enough to be the boys' father! He both protects and educates them, and is experienced enough to realise that a firm hand is necessary if you want to make it as a newcomer in this tough business.

Slater as the manager of one of today's most successful groups, enjoys admiration from colleagues in the business – and he can look forward to a secure financial future. But it hasn't always been like this.

He was born and raised in London – almost within the sound of Bow Bells. According to Terry, this gives him the right to call himself a real cockney lad!

Without any formal education, music became a way out of what looked to be a dreary existence. Little Richard and Chuck Berry were his saviours. "If they could do it, I could too, so I learned to play bass and guitar." Terry recalls.

"This was before the English music scene exploded in the early sixties. Like the Beatles, I went to Hamburg and played at the Star Club. It was a rough place. Whores and sailors, drunks and junkies. One night I was called into the office behind the stage. There sat a fat guy with a cigar sticking out of the corner of his mouth and two Dobermann Pinschers beside him. On the table he was sitting behind lay two pistols. I almost wet my pants!"

Terry was told to return to London and report to his agent's office. Frightened to death, as soon as he got back home, he locked himself in and didn't dare go out for weeks. Finally he told his father what had happened and his father went to Terry's agent's office: all they wanted was to manage Terry! They took him on, tripled his wages, and since that time he has earned his living from music.

He played in backing bands for all his old idols when they were on tour in England: Chuck Berry, Fats Domino, Little Richard, and the rest. His career really got going when he joined the backing band for the Everly

Brothers, one of the first groups to sell a million records. He stayed with them for a long time, and it was during this period that he gained much of the experience that later made him so capable of handling young talent. He saw where the money was made and taught himself everything there was to know about agreements and contracts. He found out about the exhausting work schedule and how quickly it all went downhill if you started taking artificial stimulants.

After many years on the road, in 1972 he began working in the business side of music. He became the head of the publishing division of the record company EMI in England, and wrote contracts for the rights to artists such as Kate Bush, Blondie and the Sex Pistols. Then he became head of A & R and finally Director of EMI in 1979. He was responsible for signing up names like Duran Duran, Kajagoogoo and Thomas Dolby to EMI. But his career as Director was a short one.

"Things weren't going so well for EMI, and they made some big changes. As a result of financial difficulties, people were moved into different positions. They split up our team – so I quit," says Slater.

He got involved in organising one of the Everly Brothers' reunions – a great success, but then withdrew to his farm and began to search for the one, new, big talent he could bet everything on.

Slater had many friends and contacts who were constantly recommending new groups. Every day he received demos from young hopefuls. One person who often presented him with new possibilities was John Ratcliff, who had a little studio in London that made demo recordings. And one day *a-ha* came in . . .

"Now I work a hundred percent with *a-ha* and only *a-ha*. They're the only ones I want to manage – now and forever. I've put all my personal prestige and private funds on the line for them. For me, it has got to work out. Otherwise I'm finished. I'm going to make *a-ha* into the biggest group in the world. It will require a lot of time and hard work, but I know we'll succeed. *a-ha* have the talent, songs, looks, style and magic and yet they could be the boys-next-door. They're special, but ordinary at the same time. They have some of the same personality that the Beatles had. Some go for the shy, sensitive one, others the dark one, and others the extrovert one. They appeal to everybody," explains Slater.

Terry Slater and John Ratcliff formed T.J. Management to take care of *a-ha*. Ratcliff deals with the technical and musical aspects, and Slater is the international business manager and liaison person for Warner Brothers' head office in Los Angeles.

Through Terry Slater's involvement, a secure relationship has been built up between the group, management and record company. Everyone has invested a great deal, everyone wants a profit, and everyone wants to get paid in the meantime. *a-ha*'s rapid success with their first singles and album is unique. Usually a group releases at least three albums before they begin to earn really big money. By that time, the record company has invested enormous amounts in studio expenses, promotion, tours etc . . . and a group has to achieve a respectable amount of sales before they can manage to repay their debt. Yet only four weeks after the release of *Take On Me*, *a-ha* had sold enough records to repay all Warner Brothers' expenses. So they arrived unusually early at phase two, which is where the group, the management and the record company are all earning money. As a result it became easier for Warner Brothers to invest in more promotion, new

Terry Slater, Jeff Ayeroff, vice-president of Warner Brothers and Morten get down to business

videos and more travelling.

Terry Slater wastes neither money nor confidence. He knows the results of overnight success and money burning holes in inexperienced pockets. So he has kept a tight hold on the purse-strings – sometimes keeping the boys' wallets empty while the money earns interest in the bank.

"I have accepted an enormous responsibility," says Slater. "I've taken three young boys out of their high-rises in Oslo and put them in limousines and luxury hotels almost overnight. I love them like my own children. I only want what's best for them, so I have to teach them to avoid obvious temptations. I must try to keep them from becoming too spoilt and arrogant. They have to learn how to work for success. At the same time I want them to be able to experience how much fun it can be to succeed in this business. Of course they're allowed to live it up on their own and control their own lives, but I want to warn them against the obvious pitfalls that I know, from my own and others' experience, will present themselves. If they can avoid these traps, this is a fabulous business that I know the boys will enjoy immensely. For my own sake I want *a-ha* to last. I've invested everything I've got in them, and I want a lot in return. The important thing is to steer clear of exaggeration. Not to work them to death. Not to crush their creativity, but keep the spark in their lives. Keep in contact with their homes in Norway. Keep their feet planted firmly on the ground and let them enjoy themselves along the way . . . then I know that *a-ha* will last."

78

Staying on Top . . .

Is there no stopping *a-ha*? Definitely not! The story so far . . . is just the beginning.

The boys conquered the world in 1985 with their hit singles, debut album and award-winning videos. The release of the third single in March 1986, *Train of Thought*, together with yet another sensational video, has proved to even the most sceptical of critics that *a-ha* are not just 'one hit' wonders.

The constant hard work has paid off. The first world tour (starting late Summer '86 till the end of the year) taking in America and Australia as well as Europe, has been eagerly anticipated by hundreds of thousands of fans. It will be positive proof of the boys' talent, enthusiasm and versatility.

And while many groups take time off to rest after an exhausting work load – *a-ha* have been just as frantic throughout the year. The timing of any album release is vital and it was essential that the long-awaited follow-up to *Hunting High And Low* be ready prior to the world tour. So despite countless media interviews, family and personal commitments, and business meetings, the boys still managed to lock themselves away in the studio and complete their second album.

What the boys realised very quickly was that success can be very demanding. Travelling, touring and recording are time consuming, and being on the road so much, they felt they should at least have a home base. Early in the year Mags, Pal and Morten took the decision to settle in England and set about buying homes for themselves. They even applied for British citizenship, which was great news for all their English fans!

One thing is certain. *a-ha* have achieved more in a year than many groups do in a lifetime. For that group to come from Norway makes it even more surprising and remarkable – but now they have made it to the top, that's where they intend to stay!

RADIAL